WHEN YOUR BACK'S AGAINST THE WALL

WHEN YOUR BACK'S AGAINST THE WALL

Fame, Football, and Lessons Learned Through a Lifetime of Adversity

....

MICHAEL OHER

WITH DON YAEGER

AVERY
an imprint of Penguin Random House
New York

AVERY

an imprint of Penguin Random House LLC
penguinrandomhouse.com

Most Avery books are available at special quantity discounts for bulk purchase for sales promotions, premiums, fund-raising, and educational needs. Special books or book excerpts also can be created to fit specific needs. For details, write SpecialMarkets@penguinrandomhouse.com.

Hardcover ISBN: 9780593330920
Ebook ISBN: 9780593330937

Printed in the United States of America
1st Printing

Book design by Silverglass Studio

To my wife and kids, who stood by me and loved
me for who I am, even in the darkest seasons of my life.
When there was no one else there to help, you stayed
by my side. You are my strength. You give me
purpose and love, and for that I am thankful.

Contents

Preface

It's hard to believe it was a little over a decade ago that I wrote *I Beat the Odds*. It was my first book and in it I shared my slow rise from childhood poverty all the way to the NFL draft. My life had been depicted in the Oscar-winning movie *The Blind Side*, and today, some fourteen years after that movie, it seems like you can't turn on the TV without seeing my Cinderella story. The movie turned me into something so rare it almost doesn't exist— a famous offensive lineman.

It was 2011 when as a rookie in the NFL, I set out to give *my* perspective on my own life. In *I Beat the Odds*, I shared details from my childhood so that I could be a resource and encouragement for foster kids and the parents waiting to care for them. From the feedback I still get today, I'm humbled to say that I achieved that goal and then some.

That book was about my past. This one is about my future.

When I left you last, I had no idea what seasons—on and off the field—awaited me. It was 2011 and I'd yet to become a father. Aside from my wife, football was not just my work, it was my world. I gave it everything.

During eight years in the NFL, I played for three teams and had a career of which I was proud. When I left the NFL in July 2017, I was exhausted physically and mentally. I just wanted to keep to myself and be with my family. After a lifetime of struggle that started long before I played pro sports, I'd earned time to relax.

Right?

But I couldn't. I was restless. For the first time in my life, I had what I'd always wanted: downtime. Since childhood, the only thing I could count on was the next uphill battle. As an eight-year-old, I dreamed about being an adult so I could have a moment to just chill. But once I became older, I realized that could never happen. I may no longer be a professional athlete, but I'm never going to be comfortable sitting on the sidelines. I had this nagging feeling there was more for me to do. More to my life. That nagging feeling led to a long period of darkness until I found a new purpose.

The last couple of years have made us all slow down and think. The events of 2020 had me, like everyone else, questioning everything. Widespread racial and political division and COVID-19 brought the whole world to a place of needing help and hope. The facts are real. The truth is sometimes bleak. But that's not what I'm going to talk about.

In the last few years, we've been bombarded with bad news and trapped in a world of negativity. I got through 2020, and I realized what I needed more of was *good* news. Encouragement. Positivity. We've all had our backs against the wall and it's time to find our way forward again. So, if you're ready for hope, I'm ready to give it to you. I want to talk about the light ahead, how I've found it repeatedly, and how I'll encourage you to do the same.

I've always considered myself a fourth-and-one guy. In the last-second drives to win the game—the toughest times—that's when I come alive, when my back is to the wall. It's no secret I've had a lot of walls in my life: the wall of the projects, the wall of hunger, the wall of homelessness. I've had to go up against aca-demic doubters, bullies, and athletic competitors. My life has had a lot of highs, too: a family of my own, a college education, a first-round draft pick, a Super Bowl victory, and a second ap-pearance in the "big game." But even after all these successes, I found myself in hard times again. The struggles I've faced these last few years—job loss and battles with mental health—haven't really been shared with the public.

This book was two years in the making. As I've worked through it, I've also been working through my challenges. Mak-ing a list of what I call "Back Against the Wall" principles. I've stayed committed to them, so now, like a playbook, I can share them with you when it's fourth and one in your own life and you need some encouragement.

Many of you are there right now. You're reaching behind and feeling nothing but a slab of concrete. My hope is that just pick-ing up this book is the first step away from your wall.

Before I can share those lessons with you, I must first bring you up-to-date on my life. I was only just entering the NFL when I left you last. So much has taken place since then. I see our time apart as a halftime. The part of my life that I want to share with you now can be understood as one of the most eventful second halves of any game I've ever played.

In *I Beat the Odds*, I said something that would come back to me years later: "Rough times don't have any power over me any-more; I don't have to be afraid of them because I have turned them on their head. . . . Even after you've beaten the odds, there is still room to grow. . . ."

I had no idea what "rough times" awaited me in the twelve years that followed. How my words would fall like a prophecy. The credits might've rolled at the end of my so-called movie, but that is far from the end of my story.

WHEN YOUR
BACK'S
AGAINST
THE WALL

PART I
Second Half

1

Big Oak and the Big Dream

Recently, I was invited to speak to the kids and parents at a Christian home for abused and abandoned children called the Big Oak Ranch. Even after all these years, I still get a little nervous before a gathering where the main event is me. *Why am I doing this? I'm a private guy.*

It only took me a few seconds to remember the promise I'd made to myself. For whatever reason, I've been given a platform and I refuse to waste it. But on this particular evening, I didn't have any of those feelings. On the three-hour drive down from Nashville to Rainbow City, Alabama, I thought about the kids in my audience. How I wanted to encourage and challenge them—and maybe even call them out. Most adults have lied to them more times than they can count, but because they knew my story, they were willing to give me a chance.

I hadn't spent much time in Alabama, but as I drove down the long road leading to the Big Oak Boys' Ranch, I was shocked: new, clean facilities; big brick homes for the parents and kids that were scattered around the grounds; and wide green fields. This was not the typical foster care situation I was expecting. Compared to the places I'd stayed as a kid, it might as well have been the Ritz.

More than the beautiful landscape and new buildings, it was

the people. They were happy, smiling, and already gathered in the parking lot to greet me. The kids and parents were all together, enjoying the food trucks and inflatables on a spring night. There were several big-top tents with tables underneath, and all of it, I was told, was in honor of "Michael Oher Night." No pressure, right?

It only took me a few minutes with those kids to realize there was really no pressure at all. I'm not usually comfortable with this kind of attention, but I get these kids. We understand each other. There's a bond you can't put words around, evidenced by the line that suddenly formed out of nowhere. Some kids wanted me to sign random pieces of notebook paper. Some just wanted to say, "What's up?"

Before I knew it, a couple of hours had passed, and the director of the Big Oak Ranch, former Kansas City Chiefs quarterback Brodie Croyle, gathered everyone underneath the big-top tents. I learned that Brodie's father, John, had started the Christian ranch back in 1974. He and his wife, Tee, had had a single farmhouse and five boys who needed love. From that grew a home that has helped more than two thousand kids to date.

Home being the key word. A place that's permanent. A place where kids who'd been tossed from one place to the next could memorize their address because it wasn't going to change.

Brodie climbed the stage and addressed the group. It was interesting to watch the leadership of a great quarterback be transformed into something even more powerful. After a few jokes, a song, and a prayer, he nodded toward me. "Well, I'm not going to spend a lot of time on introductions," he said. "If you don't know this man, google him. Go watch the movie. Go watch Pro Bowls. Those accomplishments are all amazing, but they're not the core of his life. Michael wanted to come speak to you tonight because at one point *he was just like you*. He wanted to share his story because it very easily could have gone another way . . . if he'd let his past be his crutch, instead of his platform. . . . So, Michael, come on up!"

I thanked him and looked out over the podium at the faces gathered around me. I'd spent the afternoon talking and cutting up with many of them. I'd watched them joking around like regular kids. The abuse, abandonment, and neglect can sometimes hide behind a smile. What gives them away is their eyes. They're grown-up eyes, and at that moment they all turned to me.

You couldn't hear anything but cicadas buzzing in the trees as I looked down at my iPhone notes. I'd spent a week preparing what to say, but I put the phone in my pocket and pushed the podium aside. This was a night to speak from the heart. The core of what I wanted to tell them went all the way back to what I'd told myself as a kid.

Like always, I started with a joke. "I'm more handsome than the guy who played me in the movie, right?"

The ladies always get a good laugh at that. But then it was time to be real. I wanted them to know every moment matters. Every day matters. I wanted some of them to hear, maybe for the first time, that they have choices. Not everything is out of their control.

"Opportunities are right here within your reach, but you can't take hold of them if your hands are full. You've gotta drop the anger. It's a weight. You deserve to feel what you feel, but there comes a time when that 'Woe is me' attitude is like sitting at a bus stop to nowhere."

I saw a few of the kids' eyes get bigger when I said that. A few of the housemothers even let out a soft "Amen."

My message is full of hope, but it comes with the awakening truth of reality. The kids in the audience that night all had it rough. I didn't need the details of their lives to know where they'd been. But if you're so focused on the bad from your past, you can miss the good right here in the present.

"Big Oak is pretty magical," I told them. "I'm going to come back unannounced next week and see if everybody is happy and smiling all the time."

I was joking, but I meant it. For the first seventeen years of my life, I would've given anything for a place like Big Oak. Besides an education, they had something there that I hadn't had—a promise of stability. "You can stay with us until you are grown." It's the first thing a kid hears when he gets to the ranch.

Those boys and girls gathered around the stage needed to know that a stable home and access to an education changes the game. Those are the foundation, but attitude is the missing piece.

"My attitude growing up was the difference in life or death. The same is true for each one of you."

I paced up and down the stage as I shared with them some of the principles of my life that had saved me.

"Choose to show up every day. Use every resource at your disposal. Meet your help halfway."

Before I knew it, my time was almost up, so I left them with one final thought. It is one I think about now with my own kids, especially when everything in our world is so immediate.

"Your mind is more powerful than you can dream at this point . . . so whatever you want your future to be, you've got to change your thoughts right now."

• • •

After it was over, I did the usual high-fives and handshakes. I hugged some of the housemoms and signed autographs. We gave out copies of I Beat the Odds, and I was humbled to see many of the teenagers go off and thumb through the pages.

The kind words said to me by fans always mean something, but many times after speaking events, I'm left wondering if I made a lasting impact. Sure, I can throw up some personal stories, but you never know what's going to hit home. They say you remember 20 percent of what you hear, 30 percent of what you see, and 50 percent of what you see *and* hear. I guess that puts me at an advantage. A dude as big as me, pacing the stage and waving his hands as he talks, has to be more memorable.

When the line had finally died down, I thanked Brodie and the team for hosting me. I was just about to get back in my truck when a young Black kid came up to me. My guess is he was about sixteen or seventeen. I could tell he was nervous, so I smiled at him and greeted him like I did everyone else. "What's up, man? Thanks for coming."

His name was Kinnedy and he told me he'd been planning to leave Big Oak. He'd been living at the ranch for a while, but had a mother and brother back home. Even though he had opportunities in front of him, Kinnedy couldn't stop worrying about his family. Like me, Kinnedy was a middle child and constantly under the stress of caring about everybody. That meant going back to a bad situation just so he could be there for them.

"But your talk tonight made me think," he told me.

I knew there was probably another reason he wanted to go back. It's a principle all kids in unstable homes instinctively know: *Leave before someone tells you to go.*

Even when you're happy in the moment, you have this reflex to run. I remember as a kid I was hospitalized and under observation at only ten years old. The system had caught up to me and realized that I had been wandering the streets homeless for over a year without any parental supervision. I knew I wasn't sick, so I just got to enjoy it. I had my own room, my own TV, and food brought to me on a tray. It felt like what I thought a vacation would be like. But in the back of my mind, I knew it would end and that the end date wouldn't be my choice.

So I broke out. I picked the lock to my hospital room door and walked straight out the front door when no one was looking. I knew if I was always the first one to leave, I'd never have to hear the words "We don't want you here."

And now Kinnedy was in the same boat. But what he was leaving behind at Big Oak was far better than a room at St. Joseph's Hospital in North Memphis.

"You can't help your mama until you help yourself first," I told him. "Take the opportunity she never got. Make something of yourself, then go back. You can help her and your siblings, but only *after* you help yourself."

He didn't argue. He just nodded.

"And if it's the streets you're missing," I added, "they're always going to be there."

Kinnedy nodded again. He knew what I meant. Those same guys will always exist. If I drove to North Memphis right now, those same dudes would be on those same street corners, doing the same things. The streets are timeless in that way. "But the opportunities," I told him, "are not."

We shook hands again, and I hoped a life was changed. I hoped he and I would keep in touch. Time would tell, but one thing was certain: my time at Big Oak had solidified something that had been in my heart and was already in the works in my adopted hometown of Nashville. I knew I wanted to do more than pop in and out of kids' lives or stand up in front of them and give them helpful sound bites. I wanted to invest in their futures. The Big Oak trip made me realize how much I had left to give, and now I was compelled to figure out how to do that.

The world is an ocean of abandoned kids. Big Oak is just one rescue boat. The statistics are overwhelming. According to 2020 research, twenty thousand kids "age out" of foster care every year. That means they go their entire childhood without ever hearing the Big Oak promise: *You can stay until you're grown.* Instead, they're left to wonder if they should bolt before someone makes them go. They're forced to exit a broken system without ever knowing a forever home.

The impact of what Brodie and people like him are doing is profound, but the need is astronomically greater than any one operation can handle. After that night, I knew that I wanted to do something similar. For weeks I'd already been hard at work, researching something that gave me more excitement than I had ever felt, even on Sundays.

I was going to make a difference. It wasn't going to be just about me or my story anymore. I wanted to make a change. More specifically, a change for the kids out there just like me. How was I going to accomplish this? That part was uncertain. There was one thing that was certain, though. I felt called to the one aspect of my story that meant more to me than any skill on the football field: *my education.*

...

Let me give you a little background on how this whole idea came to be. Like a lot of good stories in my life, it started with my best friend, Jamarca Sanford.

Jamarca is from Batesville, Mississippi, and he, like me, played football for Ole Miss. Ever since we left Oxford (the home of Ole Miss), Jamarca and I have always lived in different cities, but we regularly find a way to get together. Several years back, I went to see him in Miami, and during that visit, he wanted me to come tour AcadeMir, the charter school he'd helped with in South Beach. Jamarca's involvement with the school had started partly as a business investment with his father-in-law. I thought it was an awesome use of his time and resources. Seeing the impact in the community and meeting some of the students in the gym that afternoon made me proud of him for investing in future generations when he could have easily put his money elsewhere.

I went home and didn't really think about it too much until months later. To me, the idea of doing something with education was more like a slow revelation, not just a light bulb going off. I knew I wanted to do something with the rest of my life. I knew I wanted to be an influence. I thought about those kids. What I realized was that, for me personally, the concept of a school was just a starting place. I wanted to go bigger. Way bigger. I kept thinking back to my own life. While the education piece was huge, I needed more.

What if I could do more than own a building? What if my reach didn't have to be confined to the walls of a school?

My questions were pointing to more and more personal involvement. I knew I could write a check and put my name on the wall of some existing charity or school, but that wasn't enough. I had something that most nonprofit founders don't have—a unique understanding of these kids and their pasts. Call it a cheat sheet or a road map, my experience, not just money, was what I could offer. As overwhelming as it seemed, I knew I was being called to give a whole lot more than my name to this project.

I spent several months asking around and researching on my own, and after my experience at Big Oak, I'd settled on a similar concept: providing a place for kids who had nowhere to call home. I didn't mean that I would go buy a bunch of land in some city somewhere to build homes for a handful of the kids aging out of the system. What I wanted to do was re-create the sense of belonging that Big Oak gave to those kids I spoke to. That was a treasure I knew the value of. It was a moving part of my own story that made all the difference in my life.

As crazy as it might sound, deep down the gift of feeling wanted or accepted meant more than a roof over my head or food in my belly. I wouldn't have said that out loud at the time as a kid, but it was true nonetheless. Yes, I was starving. Yes, the nights spent sleeping in sheds or abandoned cars were terrifying. But when I think back on it, I don't think I can recall all the ingredients on my plate, whenever I had my first warm meal after going hungry. It was a meal, and I was just trying to survive. What I do remember was the first time I didn't feel like I had to run away out of fear of overstaying my welcome. As a kid whose only lesson in a bitter world is that they are alone, that no one wants them, hearing and knowing that you belong to something where other people actually care enough about your outcome to not abandon you—that is life changing. In that moment, the world doesn't seem as dark or as broken as you thought it was. That feeling opens a small sliver in the dark clouds hovering over your head. It is just enough to give you hope—to make you believe that there are brighter days ahead. That is what I wanted to re-create, a place where kids could advance their education while feeling like they belonged.

I didn't want to make another dime-a-dozen academy for the athletic and the elite. Don't get me wrong, those places are great. But this wasn't going to be about extracting athletic talent from the inner city. This was about changing lives. About echoing the Big Oak promise: *You can stay here until you are grown. We want you here. You don't have to keep moving on.*

Initially I had thought of opening a school. When I told Jamarca my idea, he laughed. "When you get something in your head, you're gonna take it to the extreme. The whole nine yards and everything!"

He was right. It was extreme. Many pro players open cigar bars or car washes. Maybe a tire store. Those businesses are expected, but a school? That's a little out of left field considering I don't have a background in education. But as I've been told a time or two, "Mike, you've got a PhD in life!"

Jamarca might joke, but he's always the first to show support. "It's a huge goal, but I'm sure you'll get it done, Big Dawg." (That's what he calls me.)

I hoped he was right. I had passion and a willingness to do the work. That was enough to get the idea out of the gate, but for an operation of this size, I was going to need help.

. . .

That help came in the form of Pastor Dale.

When Pastor Dale Robble explains a situation where all the moving parts come together perfectly, he often uses the phrase *God thing*. I guess the way we came together would fall into that category.

It all started at a weekly staff meeting at Highland Park Church in Nashville when Pastor Dale said he felt led to share something. It was a desire God had placed on his heart decades earlier, but he had never spoken about it out loud.

"I feel called to start a school," he said boldly.

The people in the room nodded, but clearly they were caught off guard. The duties of the church were enough as it is. It was a great idea, but definitely a big deal.

"It's always been on my heart," Dale continued. "I know the timing is crazy. . . ."

Crazy was an understatement. At the time, COVID was at its peak. Schools were shutting down, not opening up.

"I think we've got to reimagine the church and the ways we can reach young people," Pastor Dale said, "so I'm just throwing it out there. If you know of anyone interested in starting a school, we'd be all ears."

The next day, an outreach pastor at the church called Dale up. "I know a guy that might be interested. He comes to a Friday Bible study with me. Oddly enough, he just recently mentioned starting a school."

Pastor Dale was thrilled. "Send him to my office tomorrow at one o'clock."

The only thing Dale knew about me when I stood in his office doorway that next day was that my name was Michael. From the moment I sat down in front of his desk, he was trying to figure me out. He was easy to talk to, as pastors usually are. Our conversation was mostly small talk until he asked if I played ball. I told him I'd played in the NFL, and his eyes lit up.

"Who with?"

"Panthers and the Titans. That's what brought me to Nashville. And I played for the Ravens as well."

"The Ravens," he said, thinking. "I'm sure I know you. I'm sorry to ask, but what's your name again?"

"Michael," I said, seeing the wheels turning in his head. "Michael Oher."

"*Oher*," he whispered to himself and gave an embarrassed smile.

There are so many things that are annoying about being a "celebrity," but this part was kind of fun, watching his eyes bug out a little and the sweat form on his bald head. In his defense, I'm not the kind of guy you recognize by sight. At that time, I didn't look like the Michael Oher who ran out onto the field at M&T Bank Stadium. I'd lost a few pounds and shaved my beard, but I wasn't back down to my Super Bowl weight of three hundred pounds.

Pastor Dale leaned back in his chair, smiling. "I definitely know who you are."

We talked a little more, and while we shared a love of sports, it was clear our connection was a lot deeper than football. Pastor Dale had seen *The Blind Side*, so he felt like he knew me. It's a crazy feeling to be known for a movie. Even after all these years, I'm still not used to it. Honestly, it's a battle for me these days. Think about what it would be like if everywhere you went, people thought they knew who you were because they'd seen a dramatic big-screen movie version of your life. Your pains and triumphs. Your struggles. But I wasn't there to set the record straight. I told Pastor Dale that one thing was correct: I'd attended an elite private school while still homeless. That showed me there is still a huge gap in our education system, and I wanted to fill it.

"I don't want to just educate," I said, "I want to give kids a home." There were so many days at the elite private school when I'd hoped none of the well-meaning families would poke around too much. I tried to keep my situation to myself because I knew the minute they started calling around about me, it would awaken the system (which seemed to have stopped hunting me down). My Briarcrest days would be done. What was true for me back then is still true for kids like me today. Without a stable home, a good education is tricky at best.

I explained to Pastor Dale that I was in the earliest stages of my journey to start a school. I had taken some meetings with a church in North Nashville. I'd been on some Zoom calls with like-minded folks, but I'd yet to find just the right fit—not just a location, but the team as well.

"In Nashville, like every other big city, expensive prep schools are a dime a dozen, but they're not accessible to the kinds of kids I want to reach," I told him.

Pastor Dale knew what I was talking about. The calling that had been on his heart for twenty years was for the same type of ministry.

He thought for a minute. "Michael," he finally said, "let me tell you why I want to do this. I believe in pouring out to this next generation. Teaching them to be men, husbands, dads, leaders, and Christ followers."

He looked into my eyes like he was searching for some pulpit kind of truth. "I hear what you are wanting to do, but you don't *need* to do this. You could be living the good life on some beach right now. Never work again . . . So why? I know my why, but I don't know yours. What is it?"

I have asked myself that question a thousand times. In the past, I've talked about this feeling I had about my old neighborhood. Like I was fighting for every inch of distance I could get. But now, just a decade later, I was trying to put myself back into it. Not just dipping a toe in the water, but plunging in headfirst. The trauma of poverty is real. As much as I like to be positive and not dwell on the past, I knew I'd be dredging things up instead of letting them stay buried. A hundred bad memories would come back at me every time I heard a story about one of these kids.

"I have to," I said.

It was all I knew to say.

Later, Pastor Dale would tell me the compulsion I felt was the spirit of God in me. That even when I tried with all my might to just relax and tell myself to chill, there was a sort of discomfort, a holy restlessness given to those who are called to do things.

Before I knew it, an hour had passed, so I stood to go. "Well, you think we can do this?" I asked. "Can you help me start this school?"

"I don't think a more perfect person could've walked through this door." He smiled. "I've got a lot of respect for you and your story. I'm here to help, but I have one request."

"What's that?" I asked.

"If we do this, we've got to go after it one hundred percent."

I reached out and shook his hand. "That's the only way I operate."

I'd found my partner for the task.

...

Pastor Dale and I had started with the cart, but it didn't take long for us to realize we needed the horse. After weeks of meetings and drafting, we were just starting to get our heads around what this thing would be. The hopes were big, and the descriptions were long. We kept coming back to my situation. In my case, I was at Briarcrest Christian for three years, and despite the world-class academics, I was still technically living on the streets. Talk about having one foot in one world and one foot in another. It worked out for me because I eventually found that family support, but it was a miracle any way you sliced it. My home and school life were both important, but useless if I hadn't had them together like a lock and key. It's impossible to learn when you don't know where you're going to sleep. If I was going to go after kids like me, my solution would have to be more than just providing an education. Understanding how to meet the physical needs of these kids would be no small task. The school and everything else would have to come after that.

In the research phase, we made several trips to Big Oak and we agreed that this was the total package. Homes with loving parents waiting inside them offering support, not just physically, but emotionally. Everything worked together to help these kids grow to their full potential and find their God-given purpose. If I was going to be successful in re-creating my miracle story, I would have to deliver the total package. I had a vision for something so radical and so big that it would inevitably take all of me and what I had to offer in order to bring it to life. I knew I would have to give more of myself to this vision than I had given to the sport of football. It was a revelation that would make the feat seem impossible, if it weren't for the reason driving me to do it: the kids I saw standing in my shoes.

Honestly, there was another reason, too. There was something in it for me personally: a chance to finally have a say in my own legacy.

The way most of the world knows me is from a movie. A character that came from somebody else's imagination. Like I said to Jamarca, "What is my legacy? If I died today, what would people say when I'm gone?" In my head my hopes were that it wouldn't be about the movie or my NFL career. If I was being honest with myself, I wanted a legacy that was built around what I did for others and not one that was founded on what others did for me or what I did for myself.

And here's what I didn't say to those kids at Big Oak that day. With all due respect to *The Blind Side* and everyone who helped me along the way, it has never been in my DNA to sit around and feel sorry for myself. My story is unique, and I believe there's not one minute of it, even the most painful ones, that was outside of God's control and His grace. But I stayed positive and kept my eyes open to opportunities. When I got knocked down, I tapped into that God-given drive to stand up, to survive. The desire was the fire that kept me trying and fighting every single day.

While the movie did a great job of raising awareness about teens in foster care who might succeed if given a loving family and a chance, it did not do a good job of accurately painting *my life*. Situations get exaggerated for the sake of Hollywood. I understood that when I heard a movie was being made, but it's a strange process to live through: to suddenly lose control of your own story and to have your story written and nearly completed before you were approached for an interview. There were reasons for my silence then, but I think it is important for those who have seen or read that version to know that it wasn't just about one community saving another. It was much more complicated than that.

For the most part, my struggle and fight for survival as a kid was a solo journey. Yes, there were the occasional hands held out to give me temporary relief, but day in and day out it was just me and my own efforts. I survived the hands dealt to me from the ages of three to eighteen, before the Tuohys ever entered the scene like you saw on the big screen. Today I am once again working my way through life with my own family. When you look at that reality, you begin to realize that a better life can only exist for people like me if the individual is willing to put in the hard work to pull themselves up by their bootstraps. That's not to say that we as people are islands or that you shouldn't expect help. It simply means that the reality that Hollywood often forgets is that the rags-to-riches story they like to tell so often requires individual lifelong dedication to persistent action in the face of adversity.

That shouldn't take away from the fact that there were so many good things that came out of *The Blind Side*. For one, it gave me the platform to help people. That goodness brought by the book and movie is undeniable. I still read the fan mail I get and I'm so humbled by it. There has been so much created from *The Blind Side* that I am grateful for, which is why you might find it as a shock that the experience surrounding the story has also been a large source of some of my deepest hurt and pain over the past fourteen years.

Beyond the details of the deal, the politics, and the money behind the book and movie, it was the principle of the choices some people made that cut me the deepest. I only maintain genuine relationships as a result of the lessons I learned from those experiences. But I continue to live by the same principles that saved me from a life of adversity. I never allow myself to take too much time wallowing in the negative aspects of my life. It was my strong mind and positive, hopeful attitude that gave me the opportunity to seek that better life. That mentality has not failed me yet, and so I don't plan on abandoning it anytime soon.

There are other reasons I chose to stay silent about my pain. For one, I saw that the movie provided inspiration for so many, and I didn't want to undercut that. I want to allow that telling of my story to remain a beacon of hope for the many who find refuge in its message. By letting go of the personal hurt that accompanied the movie, I was able to free myself to focus on a future way bigger than any single story. It is about empowering kids to live a life worthy of the triumph story I lived. In my mind, my story shouldn't be so unique that it would warrant a Hollywood hit that could maintain its popularity for more than a decade. I hope to set out to ensure that a story like mine becomes so commonplace that it is to be expected. In other words, finding a way beyond adversity should be probable, not just possible.

• • •

My vision is still a work in progress, just as I am still a work in progress. The hopes and dreams laid out in Pastor Dale's office that first afternoon are still being refined today. For the people who know nothing about our project, Pastor Dale always puts it simply: "We want to provide a place for boys like Mike."

Like me.

Because of my history, everyone from old grandmas to young kids immediately has an idea of what he's talking about. But the label "foster kid" was just a part of my identity.

Like me means kids who need a break.

Like me means kids who are willing to do extra work.

Like me means kids who are hungry for opportunity.

There are young Michael Ohers out there all over the place, and they are waiting for a chance to be given to them.

There's the old saying "God never wastes suffering." I suffered plenty, but every obstacle made me uniquely qualified for this road ahead. *Like me* means my pain mattered for something. So, by the grace of God, Pastor Dale just might have been right when he said I was the perfect person to walk through his door that day. My whole life, God was preparing me for just this.

2

Back to Briarcrest

*You can't go back and change the beginning, but you
can start where you are and change the ending.*
—C. S. Lewis

It's strange to be thinking about your legacy at age thirty-seven.
I realize it's a privilege. Most folks are too busy with the daily
grind: trying to get through or get by; working and paying the
bills; providing for their families and caring for their loved ones.

I get it.

I'm in a unique place. I have time to think. For some of my
peers, particularly those who have retired early, that time becomes their worst enemy. I've heard a lot of cautionary tales.
Some people, including athletes, finish their professional careers
and start to feel lost. They've made some money and paid their
dues. So what's left for them is enjoying life. They go from one
party or vacation or new car to the next. That's good for a while,
but eventually it leaves you empty. Like once the lights over the
field go out, so does your purpose in life.

I was in that limbo for a while. After I left the NFL, I didn't
have the distractions of practice and games and constant trips to
the gym. For the first time in decades, I had the space to realize
something: *Football wasn't the final goal of my life, it was a*

vehicle to the next thing. Where it was taking me was the one place that I'd spent thirty years trying to get away from—back to my beginning.

I don't presume everyone has read my first book or knows my story. In the next two chapters, I'll briefly recap. I know there's information on the internet about me, but much of it is fiction. The most important parts of my story are the lessons within them. To understand the power of those messages, you must understand my story from my perspective. It was the truth I lived that led me to become the man I am today. They may not hold the cinematic drama of Hollywood, but they are real. To me, that is where their purpose is realized—in the truth.

To begin, you must know that I was never illiterate. I was behind in school, a result of skipping my fourth-grade year. But I wasn't a poor student, as I was portrayed. I liked school when I got to attend. There is so much about education that defined me. I hope to share those parts with you within this chapter. They are probably stories you have never heard before.

Though some of my life has yet to be shared, there are portions everyone knows. Some credit has to be given to Hollywood for that because one thing was true: my childhood wasn't easy. I grew up in Memphis, Tennessee, in a ghetto housing project ironically named Hurt Village. I was one of twelve kids. I don't remember anyone ever having a job and no one in my family graduated from high school before me. Just about every adult in my life was addicted to crack cocaine. I barely knew my father before he was killed. I was on my own from age seven, going back and forth from foster care to living on the street. I attended eleven schools in nine years. I repeated first and second grade. That's what my records show, but I can't recall a lot of things. There's a sort of self-preservation to your memories. You forget things just to avoid the feelings that go with them.

As a kid, I had more hard times than easy ones, more bad days than good. From a family standpoint, there were missed birthdays, missed games, and promises never kept. It's funny in a way to think back on that part of my life. I had every reason to keep my head down and give up all hope. In reality, there wasn't really a bright side to my life, no matter how much I tried to look for one. My saving grace came with the disposition the good Lord gave me. I wasn't one who fixated on the obstacles I faced. I was dead set on trying to find every potential opportunity I could get to improve my situation. Without anyone ever telling me it was possible, I believed that there had to be some way, somehow to get out of the projects. There wouldn't be a second that would pass where I wouldn't be on the lookout for my one opportunity to make it. My one opportunity to escape—to find my bright side. Then, as the Lord does when every door's been slammed in your face, He gives you a window. One that isn't painted shut with bars on the outside.

For me, the window came in the form of a school—Briarcrest Christian in Eads, Tennessee, just outside of Memphis. From the first day on campus, even before I'd been granted admission, I knew my life was going to change.

There are many versions of the story of how a homeless kid from the projects got into a private Christian school. In reality, I came to Briarcrest because Tony Henderson (the man I was living with at the time) was determined to get his son, Steve, a good education. Tony knew how focused I was on getting out of my neighborhood. He knew I was a good kid who was trying to help himself. I guess Tony figured he couldn't leave me sitting on his couch while his son pursued an education and a better life.

He went to private schools all over Memphis. Each time, Tony would walk confidently up the school's front steps with Steve's and my school records tucked under his arm. Each time, the meeting resulted in the same dead end, until that one day he marched into the administrative office of Briarcrest and found a school that was willing to take a chance. Not on Steve, with his decent record—but on me.

At Briarcrest, three men on the faculty had a real impact on my life and I don't think I've shared much about any of them. A lot of people were a part of leading me to Briarcrest, but there was one man who had the ultimate say: Dr. Stephen Simpson, the principal.

Recently, I asked Dr. Simpson what he remembered about our first meeting that summer before my sophomore year. It was interesting to hear in his own words about the "walls" we were facing when Tony came to his office that hot summer afternoon. Like the other principals, Dr. Simpson tried to follow the treasure map of my missing and inaccurate academic records. He found, as the others had, that the X marked the same spot: I wasn't qualified. But unlike the previous meetings, that wasn't the end of the road. "Thank you for stopping by. Now head back to the public schools, where you belong."

Dr. Simpson threw out an option—I could take courses through a local educational extension program, a home study of sorts. I could work at my own pace, building my academics in a quasi-virtual program. Then I'd come back in a year and they'd look at me again.

Dr. Simpson confessed to a friend of mine years later, "I wasn't really sure Michael would do it, but it was his only chance." It was more hope than anyone else had offered me and I took him up on it. It was going to be a lot of work and logistics to even start the program, but as we pulled out of the Briarcrest parking lot that afternoon, I knew that this was my one shot. Steve would be starting at Briarcrest in the fall of 2002, and if I played my cards right, I'd join him soon after. As I watched the big new building on the Briarcrest campus disappear in the rear-view mirror, I decided right then and there that I was going to be back.

...

I did the self-paced program faithfully for several months. But a phrase I'd heard administrators use to describe my educational shortcomings kept ringing in my head: "Michael is in a deficit."

I understood what that meant from a monetary standpoint. With each completed assignment, I tried to picture myself adding to my educational bank. But I wasn't really learning anything. I was gaining muscle memory from studying. I liked the rhythm and discipline of coursework, but I met with a teacher only once a week. It was hard for the material to sink in. I could memorize the words and repeat them back, but no one had ever explained what they meant. I was doing everything asked of me, but it was clearly going to take more hands-on help for me to catch up. You see, after living on both sides of the tracks, you learn one truth about the world. That truth is that you are who you hang around. Everyone, regardless of their motivation, will mimic the environment surrounding them to one degree or another. I knew what my future would be if I couldn't escape the projects. I was determined to seize the opportunity Dr. Simpson had given me. However, the deficit I was facing was a result of mimicking the efforts of an underfunded public education system for too long. That wouldn't stop me from trying, though. If this was my one shot, I was going to give it everything I had.

I made it a few months, trying to do the right thing and trusting in the process. But honestly, I had learned nothing. While my friend Steve was enjoying life at Briarcrest, Tony, seeing that the program was taking me nowhere, decided to reach out to Dr. Simpson again. This time, I attended the meeting.

When Dr. Simpson welcomed Tony and me into his office, he seemed pleasantly surprised to see me. Later he would tell me that his surprise came from the fact that I was the biggest man he'd ever seen.

"Michael, I see you've been working hard over these last few months," Dr. Simpson said in his deep Southern-accented voice. His smile quickly changed to a nervous look as he studied the paperwork that we had brought him. I sat on the other side of the desk, watching his eyebrows go up and down as he thought about what to do with me. Growing up on the streets, you learn to read people because your life depends on it. It sounds dramatic, but it's true. There were times when I was dependent on someone letting me stay one more night or giving me one more plate of food. I developed that intuition early and I used it often. To this day, I'm usually able to tell right away if a person is genuine or not. Dr. Simpson struck me as someone who truly cared.

He didn't have to say anything. We both knew there was a real problem. I'd been doing what he asked, but what I had accomplished mostly amounted to a show of good faith and discipline. I'd taken the prescription, but it wasn't the cure. Briarcrest was a college-preparatory school. I couldn't make up for a lifetime of poor education with a few months of correspondence courses. If he let me in, I was going to be drastically unprepared.

Dr. Simpson was a man of his word. "Well, Michael, you've done your due diligence. There will be a lot of catch-up work. And you need to know we won't lower the bar for you, but you can give it a try—at our pace. . . . Welcome to Briarcrest."

For the first time in my life, I felt like I really had a fighting chance to change my situation. My "Thank you" came out in a quiet mumble, but in my heart, I was thinking a whole lot more than that.

Dr. Simpson went on to say there were rules about transfers

and sports. They were particularly important in my situation, and I was expecting it. I had just finished a year of football at Westwood High School, a public school in Memphis, and I'd played well. I'd known the game of football long before I'd left the projects. As a sophomore, the last thing I wanted was to sit on the bench. Dr. Simpson truly didn't want athletics to be the determining factor for me. I knew this to be true from the onset: Dr. Simpson wanted what was best for my life more than he wanted points on a scoreboard for his school.

"When we get the grades squared away," he said, "then you can play."

I thanked him again. I was officially a student at Briarcrest.

• • •

Years later, Dr. Simpson told me that his decision in the office that day was his own leap of faith. At the time, he already had decades of experience in education, twenty-nine of those years in the public school system in Memphis. He had a good reputation in academics, but he was new to Briarcrest. It was just his second year as the school's principal, and he understood that not everyone on the faculty would agree with this choice to admit the kid from Hurt Village. Some might even view the decision as cruel instead of merciful, setting me up to fail. Briarcrest was a Christian school and most of the teachers were more motivated by rewards in heaven than on earth. That didn't mean they were necessarily looking for a pet project like me, but to their credit, if they were bothered by it, they didn't let me know.

Dr. Simpson would have to get approval for his decision. The promise he made took him all the way to the office of the Briarcrest headmaster, where he made the case for me: "I've given this kid hope. He's done what I asked. There's nothing for him to go back to in the public school system. He needs this chance."

The school normally would never have accepted someone in my position, but Dr. Simpson saw a desire in my eyes that made him almost uncomfortable. The headmaster, trusting Dr. Simpson to make the right call, deferred to his assessment. That's how the new principal at Briarcrest put his reputation on the line to go after the one lost sheep—me.

. . .

Everyone was right about one thing: academically, I was in the deep end. That sophomore year meant a lot of paying dues. As grateful as I was to be there, the warnings were true. I was going to struggle—big time. I came in with a 0.76 grade point average. Rock bottom of my class.

Nothing to do but climb, I coached myself.

If there was ever a time to say, "You're right. It's too hard. I quit!" it was during those first few months at Briarcrest. I didn't talk much, but my teachers saw in me the same thing Dr. Simpson did. He described me as guarded, not shy, something I appreciated as a football player.

But I was also hungry and grateful. I was going to do everything in my power to let my teachers know I wanted to be there. That determination was a choice. Character is like that; it is the one area of your life that you have 100 percent control over no matter your circumstances. I was thankful for that fact, too, because good character is often the most vital ingredient in making someone successful. Ironically, it is also something that cannot be measured by a school's grading scale. Though I may have been at the bottom of the class academically, I was more determined than my peers. Thankfully the teachers saw that.

I learned later that the faculty rallied together on numerous occasions with the single objective of helping me. I would have tutors and attend summer school. It was more work for them and for me. While I was at Briarcrest, I could not let up on anything, not even for a day.

It was the same theme for my after-school activities. Before I was technically on the football team, I stood on the sidelines. I watched, I listened, I participated as much as possible, knowing my cleats would never hit the field on a game day.

It was a good season for Briarcrest. They ended up going all the way through the playoffs and came away as the 2A State Champs in 2002. It was the first time they had won a championship, so naturally the guys were excited, and I was happy for them. When the state championship rings came in, I was officially a Briarcrest student, but I hadn't really been on the team, so there was no ring for me. Silly as it might sound, it bothered me. I wanted a ring. I *really* wanted one. Not because I'm a jewelry guy, but because the ring was a symbol. It meant you could work for something.

It wasn't my time yet, but it would be.

I'll get my own ring one day, I said to myself.

I know that probably seems crazy considering I was a straight-F student who was ineligible to play sports. I believed there would be other chances.

If I fall in love with the process, I can get there again. And the next time, I'll have the ring to show for it.

• • •

Despite how the story might have been told in the past, there was one person who was a big part of getting me in the door of Briarcrest: John Harrington, the basketball coach.

He, like me, just went along with the movie narrative. But the truth is, Coach Harrington and Big Tony went way back. At the time, Coach Harrington, like Dr. Simpson, was new to Briarcrest. It was his first season coaching basketball at a private school.

Earlier, he'd coached at Bartlett High School in Memphis. Tony had an AAU player who went to play for Harrington at Bartlett, so the men had known each other for a long time. Tony, from a sheer physical standpoint, was hard to forget. Since he was close to four hundred pounds at the time, he didn't like climbing the bleachers, so he would faithfully sit in the front row, watching the games and interacting with Coach Harrington. They knew each other well enough, but had lost touch, until Tony stuck his head in the Briarcrest office that day and surprised his old friend.

"Tony, what you doin' up at Briarcrest?" Coach Harrington asked.

Tony shared the reason for his visit, but when he stepped aside to introduce his son, Coach Harrington was confused. Steve, who was six foot one and 160 pounds, didn't resemble Tony. The three-hundred-pound kid beside him did.

"And who's this boy?" Coach Harrington asked, nodding at me.

"A kid from the neighborhood. . . . Honestly, if you could get him in school as well, that would be a real blessing."

"Well, let's see what we can do," Coach said, clapping me on the shoulder enthusiastically.

The rest of the story, you already know.

• • •

It was that enthusiasm that I will always remember about Coach Harrington. I get asked all the time, "Who was your favorite coach during your career?" That's a hard question because I've had a lot of good ones. I have a special bond with my old football coach at Briarcrest, Hugh Freeze. He was also with me at Ole Miss. We have a unique history. Not many guys get to have the same coach in high school and in college. He is a dear friend of mine to this day.

Coach Harrington was another of my favorites. He truly cared for me. I love to tease him: "The greatest lesson you taught me was to stop playing basketball and focus on football." We have that kind of relationship. I still text him on Father's Day.

...

For my first several months at Briarcrest, as promised, I was strictly a student. But as the semester progressed, my grades were slowly starting to improve. I still had some hefty academic baggage, but after the first few weeks, everyone on the faculty, right down to the janitor, could see I had a work ethic.

When word of my improvement got around to Dr. Simpson, he took a meeting with Coach Harrington. Technically, at the end of my sophomore year, I was eligible to play for the JV basketball team. It was already well into the season, but the coaches had seen me standing around in the gymnasium watching practice. It was no secret that basketball was my first love, so Dr. Simpson and Coach Harrington decided to give me a chance: I could join the JV squad for the last few weeks of the season.

The opportunity would be both a reward for working hard and a test to see if I would be able to balance sports and academics.

When I talked to Coach recently and asked what he remembered about coaching me, the first thing he said surprised me.

It had nothing to do with basketball.

"I remember when we were playing in Myrtle Beach," he said. "It was a Saturday night and we'd just finished our devotional. I asked the team if anyone wanted to share anything that was on their heart. Of course, it was a bunch of sixteen-year-olds, so they said nothing. But you simply said, 'I just want to thank everybody for all you're doing for me.'"

He still remembers it twenty years later. He knew a few of the challenges I was going through at the time. One of them being that I wasn't certain where I was going to live when we flew home the next day. I'd had a family I was staying with, but I'd sensed it was time for me to be moving on again. That transition was always tough on me, but the gratitude for what was going right in my life made the hardships more bearable.

The South Carolina trip was a milestone for other reasons. It was the first time I'd ever been called the N-word. I remember Coach Harrington going up to the officials on my behalf. "You better handle this . . . *or*"—he pointed in my direction—"I'm going to let him handle it."

I knew from then on, Coach had my back.

. . .

The greatest thing about basketball is that it was fun. It wasn't so serious. Don't get me wrong, there were some challenges for me, but as Coach said, "Michael could take anything we gave to him. The demands. The critiques."

Even though I didn't get to join until the end, I had a great season that sophomore year. The team, which started out the season losing, was able to close out strong. But just like on the football field, there was a debate about where to put me. It was just the beginning of my experience with coaches wondering: *What do we do with Michael?*

I, like most of the other kids my size and age, wanted to play guard. I like basketball because I like technique. I always joked, "Let me look good doing stuff!"

But we can't all be LeBron James, dribbling around the court, and Coach Harrington had decided early on that he should try something different with me. "I know you can shoot outside the three-point line," he told me, "but we're going to try you inside."

He told me later that the switch from perimeter to post was

what he called a microcosm of me and society. The court was like my life. I was tentative and thoughtful. If I was going to make a move, I had to believe that the move was the right thing for me. "Buy in," he said.

Coach believed in my abilities on the court. In practice, he would rear back and throw the basketball to me like it was a baseball. When I caught it without a sound, he'd act like a wild man. "See! Mike's hands are like a marshmallow! If you can't throw the ball to him, you can't play for us!"

The first game confirmed Coach Harrington's decision to put me inside. After our victory, he laughed excitedly. "No one will be able to guard you from the inside."

That's one place he was wrong. I'd yet to face a player at Brentwood Academy in Nashville named Brandan Wright.

Brandan was a high school superstar and went on to have a career in the NBA. When we played Brentwood for the first time, Coach Harrington pulled me aside. "Brandan has the longest arms I've ever seen. You can shove him out of the way, but you're not going to shoot over him."

But I did things my own way. During the game, I went up for a shot and, sure enough, Brandan swatted the ball all the way to half-court.

I did this two more times—same thing. But on the fourth attempt, I'd found my niche. I shot-faked and scored on Brandan.

"He ain't no thing!" I yelled to Coach Harrington as I ran down the floor.

That was the thing about Coach and me. We could joke. He was tough on me, but he also trusted my intuition. When I was growing up, I was rarely, if ever, the best person in the room. Usually there was someone smarter, faster, or more talented than me. That didn't mean I gave up. I believed early on that I was special. Believing in myself gave me the advantage of mental strength, and

I would use that against better opponents like Brandan. To me it didn't matter that he was taller with a longer reach. I knew that eventually there would be a moment when he would let up or slip up. That one opportunity was all I needed. I often joked that no one should ever sleep on me. If you gave me the opportunity to beat you, I was going to take it. It is what defined my whole life— seizing the one opportunity. Coach saw that approach in me, which is why he trusted me. He knew that I would eventually turn my weaknesses into strengths on the court. That bond was special.

That didn't mean I wasn't annoyed sometimes. Just like with football, the basketball program at Briarcrest was run somewhat like a college program. Players had the responsibility of making sure their uniforms were washed and hung each night and ready the next day. Again, I was learning the rhythm of life skills and what it was like to have expectations set for you. Thinking about it now, I get fired up. Having people expect something from me was like gas on a flame. I was addicted to that accountability and responsibility. I wasn't going to let anyone down.

• • •

Ultimately, Coach Harrington and I both knew that, for me, basketball wasn't going to be a long game. Coach wanted what was best for my future, so he encouraged me to focus on my second love: football.

"Michael, you're not going to be a six-foot-four NBA player. The world just doesn't work like that. You'll get some offers. Maybe it's Murray State, maybe it's Middle Tennessee, but it's not going to be what you'll have in football. You stand out on the basketball court, but on the football field—you're a star."

He knew I was disappointed, but he also encouraged me to keep letting things work together. I didn't have to choose just yet. "Keep playing basketball. It's going to help your football skills."

Basketball brought with it some recognition in my junior and senior years. The awards felt good, especially for a kid who had spent so much of his life being invisible. But those things don't matter much these days, because the discipline I learned and the relationships I made became the fabric of my character and the man I am today.

...

While Coach Harrington was working on my skills on the court, there were others who were working inside my heart. One of them was my first Bible teacher, Dr. Ernie Frey.

The new campus at Briarcrest was under construction at the time I started, so many of the classes were held in temporary buildings in the back. I remember it was cold that January of my sophomore year when Dr. Simpson escorted me across campus to one of the portables for Bible class.

When I met Dr. Frey, he looked like most of the people who saw me for the first time: surprised.

But from that first moment, I could sense that Coach Frey was a person who was truly interested in helping me. (I've always called him Coach Frey, even though he never coached me in a sport.) He could see I was a little uncomfortable in his class. The temporary buildings, like everything else at Briarcrest, were not exactly designed for me. For one, I had to duck to go through the doorframe. The desks in the portable were designed so the chair and desktop were connected. After sitting in it, I could stand up with it literally stuck to me.

I approached the situation like I did most everything else at the time. I was grateful and quiet. But everything about me stood out: my size, my color, and my economic background. I was joining a class of white kids who vacationed in Aspen, and I had never even seen a mountain.

I knew there was no changing the situation. I wasn't going to blend in no matter how much I tried, so I decided I would find a way to be comfortable standing out. Coach Frey called my determination "Michael Oher–generated inertia." (A two-dollar word that no one had taught me at the time.) I would have said it like this: *There's no way I'm going backward.*

. . .

Coach Frey didn't just boost my confidence, he was one of the first people to give me an actual gift—a Bible. As I recall, it was the first one I'd ever owned. The pages were thin and the edges trimmed in gold. For Coach Frey, the Bible was his playbook, and the way he taught from it, the stories were more real than I remembered them as a kid. All my life, I'd been in and out of church with foster parents, but at Briarcrest, the children's stories of the Bible came alive. Coach Frey taught us about prayer and what God wanted for our lives. At the time, I was a sponge. Most of the men in my community couldn't be bothered with me, but at Briarcrest there were men waiting to answer any question I had. It seemed silly not to take advantage of it.

After I'd gotten a little more comfortable, sometimes I stayed after class just to chat. On one of these afternoons, Coach Frey and I were talking about the religions of the world. He loved a whiteboard, so he got out his dry-erase marker and wrote "MAN" at the bottom and "GOD" at the top.

"Michael," he said, "all the other religions require for man to do something to please God. . . . That's a problem." He took the marker and pointed at the gap. "Christianity is different." He drew a bridge from God to Man. "It's the one religion where we weren't supposed to make our own way. Jesus did that for us."

Seeing it in simple terms like that made sense. Jesus was the bridge. *He* was the way, because we couldn't do it for ourselves. That was a message I could get on board with. Someone saying, "Hey, you don't have to do all the work yourself. Someone loves you and has done this great thing for you."

I'm not sure I had the maturity to process it back then, but it encouraged me. My whole life, everything was on me to perform, to earn my way, to earn my love.

It was also the first time I really remember someone praying for me. And feeling like they meant it.

In our recent conversation, Coach Frey updated me on where the Lord has led him since Briarcrest. He left the school a few years after I did, and in 2012, he went to Ethiopia as a full-time missionary. I always appreciated that even though his skin may be as white as his dry-erase board, he has a heart for people of color.

As I think about the kids I want to impact through my foundation, I remember a prayer Coach Frey said sometimes at the end of class: "You are the God who can do immeasurably more than we could ask or imagine. . . ."

I would see that play out in my life tenfold. When I left Briarcrest, everyone had high hopes. But God was going to do more than I could ever imagine. This school had been the start of that.

I couldn't go back and change my beginning, but Briarcrest was where I started to change the ending.

3

The Business of Football

Dr. Simpson had no idea where that first unnecessary act of kindness would take us. That just two years after sitting in his office, we'd be sitting together again, listening to coaches recruit me for their college teams. By my senior year, the cast of characters appearing at the Briarcrest football games was something that I would have never imagined. Coach Harrington had been right. Football was where I was going to excel.

In 2003, I was named Division II (2A) Lineman of the Year, and First Team Tennessee All-State. Scout.com even rated me the number five offensive lineman prospect in the country. It was a courtship that now, being a much older guy, seems to me like a dream. When you have University of Tennessee coach Phillip Fulmer and the like knocking on the door, it's pretty intense.

I wasn't 100 percent sure where I wanted to play after graduation, but I always knew I was going to end up in the Southeastern Conference. I'd grown up watching the SEC, and in my mind, it was undoubtedly the best. The SEC was where they played serious football, and from my start at Briarcrest, that's what football was to me—serious business.

Honestly, I think I would have been happy with most any team in the conference. Early on, I had my eye on LSU. I attended a football camp in Louisiana after my junior year and it was an eye-opening experience. Take a hundred kids and put them on a football field so they can prove themselves and it is quite the circus. In those situations, everyone is pushing to be in the front, trying to be the star. Trying to distinguish themselves. For me, being the person I was, I hung back, getting my bearings. That's when I heard a voice calling out my name. "Hey, Mike," then LSU coach Nick Saban shouted. "Get up here and start at left tackle."

Basically, when Saban is calling you by name, the football field is the Red Sea. Suddenly, the guys part to make a way for you. Being called out like that felt good. I got in there and did okay. At that camp I realized how much more work I could be doing. Camp was tough, and it was *hot*. I wasn't in the shape I thought I was. Briarcrest was a well-coached team, but physically, I needed to make some improvements. I left there with my head high, but I knew the very next day I would put it back down and get to work.

• • •

Football wasn't the only place where my effort was starting to show some dividends. My senior year at Briarcrest, I was *finally* beginning to see some progress. For so long, every time there was a test or a quiz, I'd ask my classmates how they did, and every time I knew where I stood—*last*.

Every report card that came out, it was the same thing—*last*.

I might have come in at the bottom of the sophomore class, but as time progressed and the tests started coming back, I was passing people right and left. I was motivated, and I was going to rise. Each quiz I took, I would pass one or two of my peers. Slowly but surely, I was holding my own. Senior year, I made all As and Bs. It almost killed me, but I did it.

My studying didn't end after graduation. There were still more credits to earn and classes to attend, but thanks to a program through Brigham Young University, the summer after I graduated from Briarcrest, I finally got my GPA where it needed to be to get me into college. I got scholarship offers from Tennessee, LSU, Alabama, Auburn, and South Carolina, but ultimately, I decided on the University of Mississippi.

...

When I got to Ole Miss, for the first time in my life I finally felt free. That might seem like a simple thing and one that is very hard for most to understand. I remember my freshman year walking across the Grove, the ten-acre plot of grass in the center of the Ole Miss campus. It was a sunny day. The breeze was blowing, and I was on my way to class. I took a deep breath and took it all in.

Finally, I belonged.

The dorm was where I lived. Classes and the football field were where I worked. There was no longer the fear of being found out, that someone would come after me and take me to some other place.

But I was free in other ways: my academic record was *finally* a blank slate ready for me to write my own narrative. Even though I thrived at Briarcrest, I still had the indescribable burden of playing catch-up from the years I had spent in failing situations. I had to do double and triple the amount of work just to get out of the red. But at Ole Miss, the page was clean. I no longer was suffering from a deficit that as a little kid I had no hand in creating. I am usually one to take responsibility for my own circumstances, but the academic record that haunted and defined me in high school was, in many ways, not my doing. Finally, it was released.

In Oxford, I could start again. New classes, new friends. I had my tutor from Briarcrest, Miss Sue, who came with me for the transition, which helped a good bit. She was a cheerleader, teacher, and friend. The classes at Ole Miss were spaced out, and maybe because of that, I found some of them not to be as challenging as some at Briarcrest.

...

While I might have had an easier time academically, football was another story. It was my first time to level up, and I was ready to get down to business. I understood there were great players everywhere. They all wanted to take my spot.

The intense competition was best represented by the practice jerseys we wore. Let's say the first team wore red. If you had a bad practice, the next day the red jersey would be gone. In its place, there'd be a blue jersey in the laundry locker. I'm a visual guy, so this was a huge motivator for me. I wasn't going to be blue. I wasn't going to be second team.

There was excitement surrounding my potential on the field, but I can honestly say I approached that 2005 season like I did that summer camp at LSU. I wasn't on my high horse. In fact, all I could see was how I had my work cut out for me.

For starters, I wasn't as strong as I should have been as an incoming freshman. I could squat, but I wasn't benching what you'd expect for a guy my size. As soon as I got unpacked, I got to the gym and started getting up my reps. I didn't want to settle for offensive-line kind of strong. I came to Mississippi wanting to compete with everyone. I didn't want to meet the expectations for my position, I wanted to exceed them. Usually, I was the only lineman in the weight room. And like I did at Briarcrest, I tried to use my difference as motivation. There I was, a big lineman, having to battle with guys who were five foot seven and 150 pounds.

One of my favorite guys to get into it with was a defensive back from Louisiana, Marshay Green. What I loved about Marshay was that he, like me, was there to *work*. We were both fierce competitors who played off each other's energy. Iron sharpening iron, or however the saying goes. But our sharpening often came in the form of good-natured jokes.

"I'm gonna have more reps than you, Mike!" I don't know how many times I heard that.

I'll admit, most of the time Marshay came out on top in our weight room competition. I don't think I ever beat him in a forty, but as Jamarca likes to tell people, "Big Dawg, he went from lifting two twenty-five to four hundred—overnight!"

Jamarca likes to make me sound legendary, but the truth is, it took a lot longer than that. It wasn't until my last year at Ole Miss that I was finally able to catch up. For the first three years, no matter what I did, I wasn't getting stronger. Whatever I was doing in the gym wasn't working for me until a new coach encouraged me to rest more between exercises. Also, nutrition wasn't really a part of our training back then. I was just going in and working as hard as I could without thinking about how I was fueling my body.

Still, with effort, I was able to make some gains. After a couple of years in, it's always obvious who is going to go on to play after college. And the odds, for once, were in my favor. It's no secret that everybody in the SEC wants to go to the NFL. Few wanted it more than Marshay Green.

We were in the weight room finishing up a set one day, and Marshay said, "Mike, I don't know what you have." He laughed. "You're not fast . . . you're not strong . . . you can't jump. You have a slow forty. Come on, man! What are they looking for?"

I knew Marshay was ragging on me because he liked me. But

it was sort of true. I had nothing I could say back to him, so I just shrugged and laughed.

When Marshay walked out, a strength coach who'd been listening to our conversation caught me by the arm. "I'll tell you what you have," he said quietly.

"What's that, Coach?" I asked.

"You can play football."

• • •

There were several of us during that time who took the game seriously. Along with Marshay, there were other players who shared the mentality I did. Those guys weren't going to rest on their natural talent. They weren't going to blow off practice. Guys like Mike Wallace, Peria Jerry, Jamarca Sanford. We were our own league of extraordinary gentlemen. We understood that football was not just a game. There was serious money at stake, and we were wanting to go all the way.

Our crew had a lot to do with Coach Ed Orgeron. When I came in as a freshman, it was Coach O's first year as a head coach. Like at Briarcrest, I was starting out with an unproven coach. It's no secret that Coach O could recruit. The joke was always that he could bring in a lot of talent, but he could also run it out. Not for any other reason than he was hard on you. He was a stickler for the rules. Not everybody could take the heat coming off Coach O's face when he was fired up about something.

He didn't just use that passion for when we had a bad game. Coach O was also a great motivator. We didn't win a lot that first season at Ole Miss, but every team we faced we truly believed we could come away with a victory. I had a lot of respect for the guy, and he had respect for me. And as long as I was respected, I would do what you asked. I would put up with the hard practices. Coach

O got a lot of mileage out of that. I remember he pulled me aside once after a particularly brutal afternoon. "You're the kind of SEC lineman I'm looking for. You're physical, and you're smart. I need about ten more of you."

This meant a lot to me. As the years would go on, my workhorse mentality would be downplayed and eventually overshadowed by something that became almost a dirty word to me: fame.

. . .

That dirty word began in 2006, when Michael Lewis's book *The Blind Side* came out. In the past, I've shared my experience with it. I knew it was going on, but it didn't affect my life in that moment, and I honestly wasn't consulted about it until the very end. I figured Lewis's main message was more about my position on the football field—left tackle—than my life.

When the book was a success, I decided to keep my head down. I thought if I continued working on my skills, I could quiet the distractions that came with the media. People would eventually see me for me and the potential I had, instead of focusing on the shock value of my poverty.

But as the months and years would attest, I was 100 percent wrong. Now as a grown man I see that kid so differently. I was so quiet, so reserved. I decided that I was going to focus on one thing: football. Serious football. Everything else around me was sidelined. I didn't want to know what Lewis said in the book or to the media. As I would learn later, when you're silent like that, a lot of times you give people license to say whatever they want about you. Things that are not true.

But even after the book came out, I was still able to enjoy my college experience. The media might have focused on the fact that I was all-SEC or all-American, but as I've said before, my greatest accomplishment was in the classroom. I made the honor roll twice during my time at Ole Miss. I would even work my way onto the dean's list before I left.

· · ·

I am a patient guy. I don't mind waiting. When people ask if I am a phone guy or a text guy, I say, "Neither. I'm a letter guy."

I've always been like this. Part of what helps the waiting is planning. I've always planned for things years in advance. Some of the greatest moments of my life I had envisioned long before they ever happened. The mental image in my mind—what some call their dream—would be enough to get me through to the next day.

There's no better example of this than the phone call I got back in April 2009. It was the call I'd been waiting almost a decade for. The call that let me know I'd officially been picked up in the first round of the NFL draft.

Much like arriving at Ole Miss, I gave myself a minute to enjoy it. It was a rare moment when I paused and enjoyed the view. The biggest of all my little-kid dreams had become a reality. I signed a five-year, $13.8 million contract with the Baltimore Ravens.

My whole teenage life had been about staying on my grind, doing what I knew was right and putting in the time, trusting that somehow, in the end, it would all work out.

Finally, it did.

That moment meant, as long as I was responsible, I would never have to fear being hungry again. That my family would always have food when they opened the fridge. It might sound dramatic, but just nine years before, I'd strolled the aisles of my local convenience store contemplating whether I should steal food or starve to death. The anxiety that comes from the uncertainty of knowing whether you will have food or not is more stress than any kid should bear.

So a few years later, to know my future would be secure was like a thousand pounds of invisible weight had been lifted from my shoulders.

It was time to play some football.

• • •

I gave myself twenty-four hours on that mountaintop, and then it was time to come down.

Even as an NFL first-rounder I woke up the next morning and started my workout thinking I was going to get cut. To say I was grateful to be drafted is an understatement. For a lot of us in professional sports, specifically those who've come from tough backgrounds, it feels good to be chosen. Not just to be wanted, but sought after. A big, loud "We want you" with a dollar sign attached. That's why so many of us get lost after retirement. We never knew the feeling of being wanted before football, and we fear not being wanted again after it's gone.

If I am completely honest, there was another reason I was ready to get after it. Here's where I might surprise you. Even though I was pick 23, the competitor in me was a little disappointed. I felt like I should have gone higher in the draft. It's a bold claim and I say it with the utmost humility. But there was another player at my position who was chosen very early in the draft. I knew that he wasn't better than me on the field. It wasn't until after the draft that I was told the reason why he was picked ahead of me. No one had any questions about his intelligence.

By the time of the draft, *The Blind Side* movie hadn't been released. Even though I'd yet to be thrown into the major spotlight, every NFL recruit taking a serious look at me would be very familiar with the book. The exaggerated trial-to-triumph story that had done a great job of instilling hope in youth was now creating doubts in the minds of those who held my future in their hands. When it came down to it, the concern was simple: some teams feared I couldn't learn a playbook.

At the NFL Combine in Indianapolis that February, I was beginning to sense the doubts, and they had nothing to do with my football skills. Physically, I had prepared and there were no surprises. On paper, my stats in the game were great. At that time, there really wasn't much else to gauge a recruit off of other than their college stats and transcripts. Social media wasn't really a thing back then like it is today. If a team wanted to know about your character, they would have to rely on the word of your college coach or hope they could extract it in a short interview. With me, they had a full book on what they thought was a picture-perfect retelling of my life. From their interactions with me, it seemed as though they thought the character of Michael in *The Blind Side* was the same Michael they were eyeing for their draft pick. It is weird to say, especially knowing there are many who dream of having a book written about them, but the book was starting to become one of the biggest unforeseen obstacles in my life.

When a team is deciding whether or not they are going to draft you, they aren't just selecting a player, they are making an investment, and a large one at that. Typically, someone who is marked for a first-round pick is a no-brainer investment. Teams are essentially guaranteed that they are getting one of the best who can play the game at the collegiate level. I would be one of those players. But there was something else standing in the way of that decision. To them, the content of the book would give them reason to question my value as an investment. References to the use of ketchup bottles being my knowledge of the game—a scene many will remember from the movie—would make many of the teams hesitant. My experience and talent on the field would be quickly overshadowed by the question of my ability to comprehend the game. I did twenty interviews with different teams. During those interviews, none of the questions I received were about football. Even at this level, after coming as far as I had, adversity was still a battle that I would have to face head-on. This time it would be in the defense of my intellect.

For those who don't know, at the Combine, players take something called the Wonderlic test. It is a fifty-question quiz that is supposed to be completed in twelve minutes. It was created by a guy named E. F. Wonderlic, and its goal was to measure math, vocabulary, and reasoning abilities. It was used by the US Navy during World War II to assist in the selection of pilots and navigators, but in the 1970s, Dallas Cowboys coach Tom Landry gave the quiz to football players. It's been a part of the NFL selection process ever since.

I took the test, same as everyone else. Even though my Wonderlic score was higher than plenty of guys there that week, I could sense that there was *still* a lot of doubt surrounding my intellect. I kept getting singled out and pulled aside for more questioning, mainly on topics that didn't have anything to do with football.

The Patriots, in particular, had a lot of questions. In the end they would trade their twenty-third pick to the Ravens, who used it to select me. Though I wasn't able to settle the doubts for Bill Belichick, I *know* I could have been set up perfectly to block for Tom Brady.

The nature of the obstacle I faced during the draft wasn't so different than the ones I faced as a kid. In the same way that I limit my time on celebrations, I do the same on the what-ifs. I never saw much reason to focus on outcomes and opportunities that had already passed. My mentality was to be real about my situation, focus on what I could control, and dedicate myself to the outcome I wanted to see in the future. In regard to entering the NFL, I figured the only way to prove everyone wrong was to get on the field. That was where I had control. That was where I could change the outcome, more so the minds of those who had doubts. But it was more than just proving people wrong. I loved football and now that love was going to help me be set for life.

4

The Ring I Did Get

When I was kid, leaving the projects wasn't going to happen by simply dreaming about working the job that could get me out of there. Instead, it would be my desire to discover what was on the other side that would be my driving motivation to do what it took to leave.

I know downtown Memphis is about as landlocked as you can get, but as a kid, I stood at the edge of Hurt Village the way some people stand at the edge of the ocean. I didn't know what life was like beyond the projects, but it was all I could think about. I believed there was more than what I could see. I had this desire in the deepest part of me. It was undeniable, and I wasn't sure how I was going to do it, but I knew, one day, I'd get out.

Sports are one out. They're a way for those of us from the inner city to go from living under an overpass to owning our own mansion in the suburbs. Athletics can elevate you. You go from ignored and invisible to running out onto a field with seventy thousand people cheering you on. That's the magic of professional football, and I don't care what anybody says: it's powerful.

My professional career didn't end the way I wanted it to, but when I look at it objectively, I achieved my NFL dream. All in, I played for eight seasons, most of them with the Baltimore

Ravens. Every game I played in, I started. Preseason, regular season, playoffs. That's one hundred and twenty-five out of one hundred and twenty-five games. I won a Super Bowl and had a second appearance in the "big game." That part of my life worked out even better than I'd planned. With the success on the field came more blessings and opportunities than I can count. In some ways, I don't know how to separate myself from football. Many of my mindsets—the very ways I view the world—have come from almost two decades of total dedication to the sport. Football has given me more than I could ever dream of, and there's not a day that goes by that I'm not grateful. My son is just now starting to play. Watching him on the field and talking with him about his technique is one of the sweetest moments in my life.

But where I am right now, football is no longer my job. I can finally let it be what it was always meant to be—*a game*. A way to escape life for a minute. Not life itself.

As a kid, I couldn't see it that way. It's hard for any kid from the projects to see it that way. Right now, as I write this, there are boys and girls on blacktops and in rec centers running drills and shooting free throws. I just recently met some of them at a Boys and Girls Club in Virginia. The "game"—football, basketball, baseball, whatever it is—is not only giving them discipline, it's giving them hope. People say the chances of going pro are a little better than winning the lottery. But to a kid from the hood, it's still a chance. In the absence of education and role models, it's just about the only chance. I appreciate the game for that reason alone, but these days, my thoughts—my time and energy—are going to go toward more effective lifelines for these kids.

With that said, Saturdays and Sundays are the days I look forward to most. It is my time to enjoy the game that shaped so much of my life.

So if we're gonna talk football, let's talk *NFL football*.

I guess for me the best place to start is at the M&T Bank Stadium, home of the Baltimore Ravens.

...

I love every team I ever played for, but I have a soft spot for Baltimore. They were the team that drafted me. My first taste of life as a pro player suited me, and I was proud to be a Raven.

They had a reputation for being a very tough, very physical team, and I loved that. It was incredible to be at that next level. Everything was new, everything was pro: the gear, the locker room, the coaches. But as much as I loved the facilities, my favorite part about being in Baltimore had nothing to do with any of that. It was the fans.

The stadium was always sold out, always jumping. I guess it helps when you have a good team, but even when we didn't play great, the fans were still crazy loud, showing their support.

Baltimore, as a city, understood me. It's a tough place. Of course, everywhere has its wealthy parts, but overall, it's just a hard-nosed, working-class city, and because of that, it made sense for me to be there. Fans took to me because of my background, and soon Baltimore felt as close as it could feel to home.

As much as I loved playing at M&T Bank Stadium, I realized I was most comfortable playing on the road. I guess that's another way I'm different from everybody else. If you can take something that's generally considered a disadvantage and turn it on its head, it gives you an edge. Like playing away games. I'd spent most of my life as a "visitor" in one respect or another, so it just came naturally to me.

Even if you don't have the home-field advantage, one thing you do have is the camaraderie of your team. One of my first friends in the NFL was a teammate on the Ravens, a center by the name of Matt Birk.

On the outside, Matt and I must have looked like the Odd Squad. Matt's a white dude. Former bodybuilder. A Harvard-educated guy. We definitely came from different sides of the tracks.

But there was a lot about us that was the same. Matt has a heart for underprivileged kids. He's a man of deep faith. A self-less person who has now dedicated his life to education with the school he founded up in the Twin Cities.

Matt was one of the lasting relationships that came out of my time in Baltimore, and when I reached out to him about my desire to do something similar, he reminded me of a good story.

. . .

When you are a rookie in the NFL, you're on everybody's list. The new guys come in thinking they're God's gift to football, so the veteran players take it upon themselves to bring them down a peg.

"When you came in, especially with you being a celebrity of sorts, we all rolled our eyes," Matt said to me over the phone recently. " 'Oh brother,' we thought. 'This kid's going to be a prima donna.' Boy, were we wrong."

In my rookie season, in 2009, Matt was one of the few guys on the team who didn't know much about my background. *The Blind Side* movie hadn't come out yet, but being the serious athlete that he was, Matt didn't have time for pop culture references anyway. Of course, that earned my trust off the bat. Matt was a mouth-shut, head-down kind of guy. In his own book that he wrote in 2014 he shared a story about the unspoken battle we had my rookie year. It still makes me laugh.

Like me, Matt has always credited his success in football to one thing: effort.

"I consider myself a low-talent guy, so to make up for it, I work."

The entire time he was on the Ravens team, his effort meant being the first player at the facility every day. Like clockwork, he was always the first in and the last out. He showed up faithfully and spent the first hour or so of his workout in silence. Until one day he arrived at 6:30 a.m., and to his surprise, there was this large lineman on the floor, stretching.

"Morning, Birk," I said.

"What's up?" He nodded at me.

It was hilarious because I could tell he was not only confused by my presence, he was a little irritated as well. I get it. For guys like us, the mornings alone are your time to get your head in the game. It's kind of like sacred space, and there I was—all up in his.

He didn't let me know it bothered him, but the next morning he showed up even earlier—6:20 a.m.—and there I was, already getting in some reps.

By the third day, it was game on. Birk peeled into the parking lot at 6:10 a.m. But again, he was in second place.

"Mornin', Matt," I said calmly.

It went on like this for weeks. From the moment I joined ranks in Baltimore, Matt could never beat me, until one day he showed up and looked around. He had done it. He was alone.

"I got him!" His laugh echoed in the empty facility.

A few minutes later, I came running in. "My alarm clock didn't go off!"

"Ohhh sure!" he teased.

But he knew I'd never let him win. I wasn't "late" that morning because I had decided to sleep in. Like Matt, I'm not a snooze-button kind of guy. Also like Matt, I've never been ashamed to let people know I have to work. Some first-rounders act like everything comes naturally, but I was never "I woke up like this" in terms of my talent.

There was another thing Matt reminded me of when we talked. A motto that the veterans (aka old dudes) said to us newcomers: *Be a pro.*

I could never forget it because we heard it over and over again. The vets were reminding us that we rookies needed to tend to detail. This wasn't college ball anymore.

"But you were a pro from the start," Matt told me. "You didn't need reminding."

When you make it to the NFL, for that first year you're drinking from the fire hose as far as the playbook is concerned. There is so much to memorize, much more than at the college level. So I did my homework. I made it my business to be prepared for every play. More than that, I studied my opponents. I learned everything I could about who I was going up against—their strengths and weaknesses. Maybe it went all the way back to Briarcrest and Coach Freeze, but I knew I needed a strategy. Birk, my Harvard guy, appreciated that I wanted to be mentally prepared.

There's an age difference between the two of us, but Matt has always insisted he wasn't my mentor. He's always treated me like a peer and a friend. When I came to Baltimore, he'd been in the league eleven years already. I looked up to him right away. I looked to his experience, and here I am now, more than a decade later, doing it again. When I told him I'd undertaken this education project, he wasn't shocked at all.

"Of course you're going to do that!" he said. "You're a doer, Mike!"

Having started a school himself, Matt has given me a fair amount of encouragement and cautionary tales surrounding start-ups in the education space.

"The journey will take a lot of time and money," he said. "There are constantly fires to put out. The best advice I can give you for this endeavor: Be humble. Ask questions. Getting it off the ground will take work. Because you're dealing with people, that work will never stop. It's a grind. But it's worth it. There's nobody who knows how to grind better than you."

Matt is a doer himself. Since retiring from the NFL, he's put all of his time into projects benefiting others. In 2011, Birk received the Walter Payton NFL Man of the Year Award for his efforts in promoting literacy for at-risk youth. Today, he's a pillar in his community, a devoted husband and father of eight. My guess is with all those kids, he's getting to the gym even earlier than me these days.

...

With good coaching and good teammates, it was a good first year with the Ravens. I started every game in 2009, eleven at right tackle and five at left. I played right tackle in my first post-season game against the Patriots. We won, 33–14, and I did not allow a single sack. I was second in the voting for the Associated Press's NFL Offensive Rookie of the Year Award.

And this early phase of my career is where I left you last. My book, *I Beat the Odds*, came out in 2011. I'd already had two successful years in the NFL. I had my challenges, but I was feeling good about my career. I had a plan. The life I'd sketched out on the abandoned blacktops outside of Hurt Village seemed like it was actually going to pan out.

I had no idea what lay ahead.

....

During my first three years with the Ravens, if you asked if we had a chance to win the Super Bowl, my answer would have been a resounding yes. It wasn't just some mirage in the distance. We'd been close each year. We had good coaches. We had Hall of Fame players. But somehow we kept coming up just shy of the goal.

My second year, we had a heartbreaking loss to Pittsburgh at Heinz Field that kept us from advancing. We were up, 21–7, in the third quarter, only to lose the game in the final minutes. The next season, in the AFC Championship game against the Patriots, we were holding our own. Our defense did a great job of forcing field goals. My old teammate from Ole Miss, tailback BenJarvus Green-Ellis, aka "the Law Firm," had a great game, rushing for almost seventy yards, which was impressive given the strength of our defense.

But in the fourth quarter, things started to fall apart. We dropped a pass in the end zone and then shanked a thirty-two-yard field goal that would have tied the game. The Patriots came away with a 23–20 victory and were on to the Super Bowl in Indianapolis. We were headed home.

If you don't know how deep the rivalry is between the Ravens and the Patriots, let me tell you, it's deep. Some Ravens fans still call that AFC game one of the toughest losses in Baltimore history.

The 2012 regular season was a good one, but which two teams would make it to the Super Bowl was still anyone's guess. We had a decent record. We'd managed a few injuries, and by the end of the regular season, we were 10-6 and seeded fourth heading into the playoffs.

There were some emotional elements at play that season. The first was when former Ravens owner and founder Art Modell passed away in September of that year. To commemorate him, we all wore an "Art" patch on the left side of our jerseys for the entire season. But we weren't just losing Art. Turns out, we'd have to say goodbye to another Ravens icon.

While preparing to take on the Colts in the playoffs, Ray Lewis, a living legend on the team for seventeen years, had an announcement to make.

"This is my last year," he said.

Instantly, it was like the air got sucked out of the locker room.

To say goodbye to a player like Ray—the definition of a Ravens icon—was going to be tough. Each year, I had looked at guys who were key pieces to our team, players like Ray and Ed Reed and others who were getting up in years, and wondered: *Is this the season he's going to hang it up?*

Of course, we'd known Ray had to leave sometime. He'd been with the team since 1996, part of its original roster. The OG Raven. But when he finally said it out loud, it hit us hard. His leadership on the field and his dedication to his teammates was a stabilizing force. It's like the old saying, "When a great tree falls, the forest is never the same." The landscape of the Ravens organization was going to change forever.

I came up to Ray afterward. "Man, I thought you were gonna retire when I retired!" I laughed.

It's no secret that professional athletes are superstitious, but they are also sentimental. Sports are a head game, and that emotion sometimes gives you an edge. I knew, and Ray knew, his impending retirement was going to put a fire in all of us. This news was the motivation we needed to take us to another level. Those of us in the locker room that day all made up our minds that the tree wasn't just going to fall, we would make sure Ray went out like a champion.

From that moment on, we were locked in. For Ray, if nothing else.

....

Going into the playoffs that 2012 season, I prepared to do the extra work. I studied the tapes. I was the first one in the building and the last one to leave. I could not get enough prep, knowing I'd have to be ready for future Hall of Famers like Robert Mathis and Dwight Freeney, two defensive all-stars for the Colts.

We had faced the Colts in the playoffs twice before, and both times, we won. The AFC wild card playoffs would be Ray's last at M&T Bank Stadium, so we were all determined to lock it up.

The scoreboard reflected that. Our defense won the day with three sacks and two forced turnovers. Anquan Boldin, our best receiver, had over 140 receiving yards, setting a franchise record for a postseason game. Thanks to our defense, the Colts didn't get a single touchdown. We came away with a 24–9 Ravens victory.

On the last play of the game, we put Ray in at fullback for one last kneel-down. After the clock ran out, Ray broke out into his dance, but he didn't get too far into it before we all swarmed him, hugging him and congratulating him.

After the game, Ray said to the media: "I knew how it started, but I never knew how it would end here in Baltimore. To go the way it did today, I wouldn't change nothing."

Our celebration time was quick because it was on to Denver to face the top-seeded Broncos. They had beaten us, 34–7, just three weeks before, but still, we had some good momentum, and most people were expecting a decent matchup.

That game in Denver turned out to be crazier than anyone could've predicted. Later, *Sports Illustrated* would call it "One of the most exciting and entertaining postseason games in NFL history."

Three returned touchdowns, twenty-eight points scored in the first eleven minutes, five lead changes. Not to mention it was *bitter* cold. Joe Flacco threw a seventy-yard bomb to Jacoby Jones, tying it up with under a minute left to play. After that, the game had a new name: the "Mile High Miracle." I don't care what your religious background is, you see a play like that and you have to believe! Peyton Manning and his Broncos were heavily favored, but we fought them all the way into double overtime. Our rookie kicker, Justin Tucker, made a forty-seven-yard field goal, and we came away with a 38–35 win.

For me, that game was a personal victory. Leading up to it, I had done my homework. That meant getting familiar with my opponent. Watching tape. I had one worry: Von Miller.

Von was a one-man wrecking crew. He had something like twenty sacks that year alone. He was almost winning games by himself. The thing about guys like Von is that they're fast, but they're also surprisingly strong. Von could put his hand on you and lull you to sleep—it was almost like one of those WWE wrestling moves.

Before the Denver game, I watched his film for about six games, constantly rewinding, studying his form. He was the best pass rusher I had ever seen. But then it hit me. My preparation was actually taking me backward. It was late at night, and I looked around the empty room. I realized I needed to shut the tape off and go home. Get some sleep. If I kept watching, I was going to be terrified going into the game.

Players like Von Miller could get in your head, but I knew a secret. Defensive ends were all about reaction. I realized if I could win off the snap, attack him, I didn't even have to do much after that. I knew with Von, if you waited on him, you were giving him the advantage, so I was going to initiate contact before he hit. Basically, attack. Force him to play off me, instead of me playing off him.

My instinct proved right. Miller wasn't used to seeing that kind of aggression. And for me, that victory in Denver wasn't just physical, it was mental as well.

People have asked me a few times what I would consider the best game of my career. Was there a moment when the preparation and the grind and everything seemed to pay off?

The Mile High Miracle is my answer. For me, it was as good as it gets.

...

After the epic victory in Denver, it was back to Gillette Stadium to face the Patriots. For us and New England, it was like *Groundhog Day*. There we were again, facing off in the AFC Championship.

The Patriots were leading, 13–7, at the half, and I have to admit, I had a pit in my stomach, feeling like history might repeat itself.

But our defense came through. We didn't give up a single point in the second half and pulled off a 28–13 victory. That game marked a few firsts for the Patriots. It was the first time a road team had beaten them in the AFC Championship. It was also the first time Tom Brady lost at home after leading at the half.

Again, the Ravens-Patriots rivalry is intense. That bitter competition is the good stuff. It's pro football at its truest and best. So to win the AFC Championship, especially after the loss the year before, was very sweet. This time, the Patriots were sent packing and we were the ones headed to the Super Bowl.

...

In a way, going to the Super Bowl is like becoming a parent for the first time. You can imagine what it's like. You can watch it happen to people on TV. But you just don't know it until you go through it yourself. The pain and the glory.

The team was founded as an expansion franchise in 1996 and has qualified for the NFL playoffs fourteen times since 2000. It has appeared in two Super Bowls. The first Super Bowl led to a title back in 2000, and the second appearance was with me. I'd only been in the league for four seasons when I got my debut in the big game. Our opponent for Super Bowl XLVII was a more seasoned franchise, one of the most respected in the NFL—the San Francisco 49ers. At the time, they had appeared in five Super Bowls—and never lost a single one.

There were other reasons that made Super Bowl XLVII special for everyone, not just our team. For one thing, it was cool to have New Orleans hosting it again at the Superdome. The city has a long history with the Super Bowl, but that year was their first since Hurricane Katrina.

It was also the first time in league history that two brothers were coaching against each other in a Super Bowl. Our John Harbaugh against their Jim Harbaugh, John's younger brother by fifteen months. The media and fans had some fun with that, giving the game endless nicknames like the "Superbro" and the "Har-Bowl."

I didn't have a brother in the game, but my buddy from Ole Miss, Patrick Willis, was playing on defense for the 49ers. Patrick is legit. At that time, he was All-Pro every year. But more than that, he's a good dude. It was cool to have somebody who had my back, even if they were on the other side of the line of scrimmage. He and I have always understood each other, even though he calls me "Grizzly Bear." I'd like a smoother nickname than that.

"Man, I don't want to be a bear! My end-game physique is lean and mean!" I always joked with him.

Even when you're used to playing at the highest level of the sport, the Super Bowl is on another plane. Whenever you are being watched by more than a hundred million people, the pressure is pretty intense. But at the start of the game, it seemed like everything was falling our way, and going into the half, we were feeling pretty good. The score was 21–6, and with that kind of a strong lead, some folks were predicting a blowout.

Turns out, Patrick and I weren't the only reunion that day. During the halftime show, Beyoncé sang "Halo" and "Single Ladies" with her former Destiny's Child bandmates. The show was supposedly one of the most watched of all time. But obviously, we missed that one. We didn't see those $4 million television commercials, either.

The real show came after the half. With thirteen minutes remaining in the third quarter, the stadium went dark.

You'd think in a moment like that, people would scream, but what was even more eerie is that for a split second, everybody in the Superdome went quiet. It took us a moment to realize what had happened. A partial power outage cut the lights, bringing the game to a screeching halt. Then there was this kind of excited roar and chanting. Half the power in the stadium went out in almost a perfect semicircle, taking out the scoreboard.

It goes without saying that you never get a break in an NFL game. Even in bad weather, the field is cleared and, somehow, play resumes. So that kind of pause during the biggest game of the year was unusual, to say the least. As soon as the lights went out, I started to worry.

"This is not good," I said to myself. I had a hunch the unexpected downtime was going to force a shift in the dynamics and cost us the game.

Momentum is a weird thing. You might not be able to measure

it in a quantifiable way, but in football, it's as real as the law of gravity. Once it's gone, it's gone. You get cold. The balance shifts and takes everything with it. The adrenaline. The power. Suddenly you're just waiting to lose. It's like when you're having a bad dream—and you know you're dreaming—but you can't seem to wake yourself up.

Sure enough, when the lights flicked back on and the fans started cheering again, what I predicted started to play out. Colin Kaepernick, the 49ers quarterback, and his receivers—Michael Crabtree, Vernon Davis, and Delanie Walker—must have gotten their wits about them during the break. Basically, when the play resumed, the 49ers showed they weren't going to go down without a fight. With some post-blackout momentum, by the end of the third quarter, they'd cut our lead down to five. We held our own and managed to pull out the victory that day with a final score of 34–31, but some critics claim that the blackout saved San Francisco from what could have been one of the biggest blowouts in Super Bowl history.

...

I have lived a lot of lives in thirty-seven years. Any success I've had has been a gradual rise. Getting out of Hurt Village. Getting accepted into college. Getting drafted. Each of these moments is a milestone in my memory. Each of them was years in the making, though it felt more like lifetimes.

But no accomplishment took as long as getting the Super Bowl win that day.

There's a picture I have from after the game, and when I look at it, I think my eyes sum up everything I was feeling in that moment. Like people say, in those pinnacle moments, time slows down, and for just a second, you take it all in. You're surrounded, not just by confetti, but by a roar of cheers. Everybody is hugging everybody.

Ray Lewis was done, and he had finished strong: seven tackles, four of them solo. But there was one thing he hadn't told anyone. He'd injured his tricep in October of that season, but the night before the Super Bowl he tore it again. But pain was not going to keep him from missing the Super Bowl. Later in a Ted Talk, he said that the night before the game, he'd tied a shoestring to his arm and secured it to the ceiling, just so he could fall asleep. That right there was why I respected him. Whatever it took, he was going to get it done.

After a Super Bowl win, you ask a player what he's going to do to celebrate, and the response is always "I'm going to Disney World!" It's probably no surprise that I didn't do anything drastic. Win or lose, I like to be by myself and internalize things. Take it all in. My wife and I are homebodies. Usually after a game—even a big win—our tradition was to go grab some food and watch a show on TV. *The Walking Dead* was one of our favorites.

I'm the kind of guy who wants everybody to be a part of everything. If I consider you a friend, I want you to feel what I'm feeling. I want you to share in any success.

But you win a Super Bowl, and it is hilarious how many people want to hit you up. Your phone blows up. Folks you haven't heard a peep from in fifteen years are all of a sudden giving you a shout-out.

I'm like, "Terrance, I haven't seen you since freshman English at Ole Miss, and here you are asking me what's up!"

There was one text that I couldn't wait to respond to. Dr. Simpson, my high school principal from Briarcrest, sent me a message: *Congratulations on the win. I'm proud of you.*

In the locker room, with all the guys going crazy in the

background behind me, I typed back: *Thanks, Dr. Simpson. This is for you, for the chance that you gave me.*

It's crazy when moments like that come full circle. I might have missed out on that first ring way back at Briarcrest, but thanks to some support, I sure didn't miss out on the second.

5

Seasons Change

They often say that life has its seasons. There are times you can find yourself on the mountaintop and there are times you can find yourself buried in the valley. If there was a life that could stand as a testament to the extreme swings of those seasons, it would be mine. All of that may be true when discussing the blessings bestowed on you, but I am not one to support that perspective.

On paper, I was extremely blessed. My adult life had been spent on the mountaintop. You learn to be grateful for that kind of blessing when you spend most of your childhood having nothing. But even with all those riches and accomplishments, I was still Michael. The kid who had grown up in Hurt Village had in many ways not changed.

My rise to the top was a journey I made by earning every step I took. It was a long climb. One that very few ever make. Looking back, I would have to credit attitude and mental strength as the necessary companions that helped me get to where I am today. When you fight your way from the bottom, you can't spend much time obsessing over the pain or struggle of that climb. If you do, you will only have yourself to blame for your defeat. The way I saw it: *Life is already tough enough. I don't want to sit in this pain any longer than I have to.* What I mean by that is simple. I knew the challenges I faced. I made note of where I was, and then I set my eyes and mind on where I wanted to be. From there, you move forward.

I went from the streets of Memphis to the Super Bowl. I became a champion. That was about as high as you could get. Finally, I was at the mountaintop. But at some point I was going to have to come down. I knew that better than anyone. The seasons never deterred me. Rain or shine I was always going to be myself. You see, I learned early on that gratitude and adversity were the two constants of life. No matter where I found myself, whether that was starving in an abandoned shed or holding the Lombardi Trophy, I always had something to be grateful for and an obstacle to face.

At this point in my life, I knew what to be thankful for: my family, the victory, my career, financial stability. Yet, it was the first time I struggled to see the obstacle. *What challenge awaits me next?*

That storm would begin to reveal itself on the horizon of my fifth year in the NFL.

• • •

Changes beget changes. It would start during the 2012 regular season before we knew we were going to the Super Bowl. I'd played sixteen games at left tackle, but I would be finishing the season at right.

My dexterity allowed me to be a team player. Whenever the team had a need—when there was an injury or someone couldn't hack it—whatever the bind was, I would be the one to help us out of it. The coaches were well aware of this ability of mine. They made sure to use it to the team's advantage, no matter where I played. If I remember correctly, during all eight seasons, I started at a new position almost every time. Rookie year, right. Second year, left. Third year, right. Fourth, left. Fifth, right. Sixth, right. Seventh, left. Eighth, left.

To those who don't play football, that might sound like no big deal. Like moving your desk from one side of the office to another. But it's actually a huge change, both mentally and physically. When you're at that level, you train more than you do anything else. More than you eat. More than you sleep. You do this so that you can have muscle memory. So that your body's reaction will be faster than your mind's ability to process what's happening. That repetition, particularly as it relates to footwork, is key. That is even more true for the position of tackle. The side of the line you play is what determines which leg is your strong one. Every lineman has their power leg that they drive their body off the line with. The back-and-forth would mean that I wouldn't have the opportunity to build my strength in a single leg. From the team's stance that wouldn't be much of a cost, but for me it meant sacrificing some personal goals.

The NFL is a level of play that attracts winners. Athletes determined to be the best. I was no exception to that. My ultimate goal was to become a Hall of Fame tackle. However, an accomplishment like that is a singular achievement. It's a goal of the individual, and football is a team sport. I understood that better than most. Surviving on my own for so long as a kid made me appreciate the nature of football. The sport brought with it the aspect of working together as a team. It was one of my first experiences of belonging. Through the game, I saw the immeasurable value of overcoming obstacles and achieving goals as a team. That lesson was one that I wouldn't abandon, even in the NFL. After all, I was hired to "play for a team, not for myself." That phrase would take on a whole new meaning at the beginning of the 2013 season.

....

The team roster would add more than just a few new coaches or players in the final year of my rookie contract. In the same year I would become a Super Bowl champion, I would also become a dad. It was a personal twist to the end of one of my most successful seasons that would blow my heart completely open. Of all my accomplishments in life, being a dad is the one I am most proud of. It takes on a whole different meaning, especially for the men who never had one to model after.

My son was born in June of 2013. After only twenty-seven years on this earth, suddenly there was a person who had no idea of who I was or who I was supposed to be. Someone who just loved me for me. In our lifetime, there are few people we can really say that about. Friends and fans can both be fair-weather. But I knew instantly that the little guy in the palm of my hand was going to be with me for the long haul. I thought about Coach Harrington and what he had said about my hands. How they were strong but soft. They were meant to hold on to things. There was never anything in my life I wanted to hold on to more than this little man. Like many first-time parents, I was obsessed.

Although my son's entrance into this world was totally different from mine, there was one way he was like a chip off the old block.

He was early. Very early.

My wife, Tiffany, and I are planners, so we'd been ready for our son's arrival long before his due date. But like his old man, he decided it was better to be early than late.

We were at Sinai Hospital in Baltimore, and I remember looking down at him for the first time. He was so incredibly tiny. Since he was born eight weeks early, he only weighed about four pounds. I have a picture of him lying there in my palm. Not much heavier than a football and definitely not as long. He had on the tiniest diaper I'd ever seen in my life. He looked so much smaller against my hand. They took him to the neonatal intensive care unit, which was standard practice for a baby his size. But honestly, I never worried about him because I knew he was special. It's hard to explain, but I could see it when I looked at him. He was small but strong. He had the fight. When his dark eyes looked up at me, he was saying, "I got this."

I might have been a homebody before, but once we got him home, the whole center of our universe was at the house. At the time, I was enjoying football. I liked being able to travel places with my friends and have a good time. The travel part of the NFL was secondary to the prep, but when we got to a new city, I always tried to squeeze in a few sights when there was time. When my son was born, everything changed. My life was centered around him: his feedings, his naps. I did everything that was expected of me, like always, but I couldn't wait to get back to the house. He became my biggest treasure.

...

As my rookie contract was winding down, I was starting to feel like maybe it was time to make a change. I am someone who is always moving. The people who know me say that I won't ever let grass grow under my feet. In a way, I know they're right.

With winning the Super Bowl and becoming a dad, I was beginning to feel like I was on a winning streak. As great as that sounds, it, to a point, unsettled me. The man I made myself into was someone who was born in the fires of trial. I liked the odds of a challenge. That kind of environment pushed me. I am still that way to my core, but even those virtues can change. If I was going to succeed, it was going to be for my kid. I began to view everything in my life through the lens of a father. That was no different with football.

Being a father pulls you home. Baltimore was great, but it was cold in the wintertime and was a plane ride from Tennessee. Even though I'd committed my childhood to escaping the projects, Tennessee was and will always be considered my one true home. I knew my options would be opening soon, and I didn't want to waste them.

Of course, there was another reason I wanted to make a change. *The Blind Side* movie cast a wider net of influence than I had initially thought. I was already with the Ravens before it hit the box office. Things were as normal as they could be for an NFL player back then, but everything would change after its release. The movie and the story it portrayed would land front and center. Every news article that came out was no longer about my performance on the field, it was about the movie. Everywhere I looked there was talk about it. You would have thought that I had made the highlight play of the century with how much my name was popping up in the media.

All the attention was more than I wanted. I am naturally a reserved guy. Seeking attention or accolades just isn't my thing. My focus is typically on the task at hand. I love getting to bury my head in something and get to work. Football provided me that outlet of dedication. At first, I figured doing just that would be all I needed to escape the media frenzy surrounding the movie.

As I said in the beginning, for most other positions on the field, the spotlight from the media might not have been such a bad thing. But I was an offensive lineman. Nobody knows an offensive lineman. Nobody is supposed to know offensive linemen. If you know an offensive lineman, he's not doing something right. By the end of that first year, suddenly everybody knew me, even the referees. They'd walk up to me in the middle of a game. "Hey, Mike, what's up?" For many in the industry, they couldn't separate me from the movie. That is probably why I took so heavily to the compliment Chris Collinsworth, an NFL commentator, paid me while he and Bob Costas were commentating during a Ravens game. He said, "This guy earns everything he has accomplished."

That meant so much to me. It was one of the few moments in my time with the Ravens that I got the nod I needed. Being recognized for your hard work is something we all strive for. Having the culmination of all your efforts and sweat acknowledged and complimented just feels good. That, however, was becoming more difficult to get. No matter how hard I worked to improve my game, the comments stayed fixed on the movie.

And after five years of it still going strong, I began to think that more dramatic measures would be needed to step out from under the shadow it cast over my football career.

• • •

On March 14, 2014, I signed a four-year $20 million contract with the Tennessee Titans. I was excited about the transition. The team felt right. Nashville felt right. It was the first city I'd visited outside of Memphis (during that game against Brentwood Academy, when I faced off with Brandan Wright). Tennessee is home to me, and I liked the idea of Memphis being just three hours away. I was going to play football in the South again. The home of the SEC. Southerners love football, so I thought maybe the Titans would appreciate what I had to offer more than some other teams.

Going into it, I liked where the Titans were at the time: in transition. Their 2013 record was 7-9, but with Ken Whisenhunt coming in as the new head coach that year, the organization was hoping to change philosophies. Establish a winning culture. To do that, they'd brought in some other veteran players like linebacker Wesley Woodyard and running back Dexter McCluster.

Woodyard is a solid leader on any team, and Dex, my former teammate from Ole Miss, is as hardworking as it gets. Dex is a small dude, but he could blow past the big guys. Some of us in Oxford joked that he must have angels protecting him, like an invisible force was knocking down the guys all around him. In addition to his run game, Dex was also known for being upbeat. You need those kinds of players to change a culture, so I was excited that the Titans were choosing quality guys like that.

On a personal level, I was in the mindset to be positive. That didn't mean that I thought it was going to be a cakewalk. No matter what your accolades are as a player, when you join a new team, you're expected to prove yourself to both your teammates and coaches. I didn't mind it. It was the kind of motivator that lit a fire under my butt.

I hit the ground running in the preseason in Nashville. Looking back, I might have hit it a little too hard. In my eagerness to prove myself to the new team, I began to experience the first of many injuries. In a preseason game against the Saints, I tore my bicep. A bicep can tear two ways. For me, it rolled into the top of my arm, but I could still manage to do what I had to do. It was a painful injury, but one I could play through.

I started the first eleven games with the Titans, but during the course of the season, I began to experience a debilitating toe injury. Basically, the damage was to the ball of my foot, the first metatarsophalangeal (MTP) joint. "Turf toe" is what they call it because they started seeing the injury in football players after the invention of Astroturf in the 1960s. With turf toe, the big toe gets hyperextended, causing pain to the tendons and ligaments, even the bone. There are a lot of professional athletes who've been diagnosed with turf toe—Tom Brady and Deion Sanders are probably the most famous among them.

My sixth year in the league, at age twenty-eight, I finally

started to feel what I'd been asking of my body. Like I've said, pushing yourself to the max every day can age you fast. And the people in high places start to look at you like a used car, wondering when an axle boot is going to bust, or praying the transmission isn't going to go out. I knew this. I'd seen the looks on the coaches' faces, but in the past they were directed at the more veteran players. I am a pleaser, not a complainer, so this was a tough spot for me. I just wanted to jump back up and get to work, but for the first time, this was an injury I couldn't play through. I couldn't will myself to fix the problem.

There's an old saying that goes "It's mind over matter." Well, I'd been doing that since I was a kid. Dr. Simpson often shares a football story from my time at Briarcrest. We were playing an away game in Murray, Kentucky, and my hand got caught in a face mask. I basically split the skin between my fingers (what some people call the "webbing" in your hand), and still, I didn't want to be taken out of the game. I stood there on the sideline, holding a bloody towel to my hand. I waited until after the game and went to the local ER to get it stitched up.

That's who I was. I didn't want to cause a problem, I just wanted to get after it.

But the toe wouldn't let me. It's such a small thing, but it was my leverage. As a lineman, people don't realize the leverage you've got to create, so without a working toe you can lose your strength. It reminded me of the Aesop fable where the mighty lion was immobilized by a small thorn in its paw. It was a new territory for me. Almost every struggle I had found myself in, there was usually some way out. Finding what it was that I could do to control the situation came naturally to me. With this, there was nothing I could do. It was an injury and I had to give it the proper time to heal. That becomes even more difficult when you are in the middle of an NFL season.

Unfortunately, like mine, Coach Whisenhunt's first season didn't turn out like he had hoped. The Titans finished out the 2014 season with a record of 2-14.

That misfortune would follow me into the close of the season. Along with the toe injury, I hyperextended my knee and, finally, I had to surrender. It was going to require surgery. I started at right tackle for the first eleven games, but on December 13, they put me on injured reserve, and I had to sit out the last two games of the season. On February 5, 2015, the Titans released me after one season.

I'd be lying if I didn't say the loyalist in me really wanted to stick around and have a chance to play in Tennessee while I was healthy. But it was a business decision, and I looked at it like that. There is always room for personal responsibility. Also, I had to ask myself, "Was there anything I could have done better?"

I could have avoided injury, but ultimately my injury wasn't on them, it was on me. They paid me some money for my time, and that was that.

What I did learn from that one season was that I liked being one of the older guys. Like Birk did for us, I could look at the guys coming in and encourage them: "Be a pro."

Even though my time was short, I hope I was able to make an impact. Lessons like the seriousness that the game requires. Like showing up on time. Like taking care of your body. These lead-by-example attributes are what I wanted to leave on LP Field. I might have had a short-term relationship with the Titans, but Nashville and I were together for the long haul. It would later be the place where I'd put down roots and raise my kids.

The Titans were in the rearview, but I knew I still had a lot of play left in me. I had a plan for my road to recovery. It was on to the next thing.

....

It wouldn't be long before I was back in the saddle again.

There were several prospects, but the interest from the Carolina Panthers had my attention. I liked their general manager, Dave Gettleman. He seemed like a decent guy, at the helm of a reputable organization. The Panthers in general had a reputation for taking care of their players. In the NFL, you can pay players to keep them. That's one way. Or you can just be good to players and maintain a certain level of loyalty and player retention, and to me, it seemed like that was how the Panthers operated.

I had yet to finalize my decision when I got a phone call. It was a former offensive line coach of mine from Baltimore, John Matsko. He was let go by the Ravens after the 2010 season and picked up by the Panthers the next day. Matsko knows his stuff, inside and out. He's still one of the smartest coaches I've ever been around. He, like me, always emphasized technique.

When we talked on the phone, it was effortless. Easy. I didn't need to remind him that, just two years before, I'd had my hands on a Super Bowl trophy. In fact, he was mad that he'd just missed out.

He said he had one simple question: "Do you still want to play football? Injured guys just walk away sometimes."

I knew he was right. But that wasn't where I was. I told him my toe was healing. I still wanted to play. I was still determined to play.

After that phone call, Matsko must have given everybody on the Panthers team my cell, because Cam Newton and four or five other players started calling me, telling me to come and join up.

It was encouraging, especially since I had just been cut. The guys said things like "We need you here. We want you here." You would have thought I was coming off a Pro Bowl year based on what they were saying.

GM Gettleman told the media, "We did our homework on Michael, and we feel very strongly that he can be an answer for us. He'll be inserted at left tackle, and we'll go from there."

In March 2015, just a month after my release from the Titans, it was a done deal: I was officially a Carolina Panther.

. . .

Taking control of my own reactions has been a key part of my success. However, I'll be the first to admit: I am an emotional guy. I take that emotion with me onto the field.

Relationships with teammates are important to me. Right off the bat, I had a bond with quarterback Cam Newton. Joe Flacco is a super-talented guy, but Cam is in a league of his own. He was like a Marvel character. He could do anything. After the first practice, I thought, *He's seriously one of the X-Men.*

There are many benefits that come with being famous and finding yourself under the spotlight. There are some personalities who are even born for that attention. I'm sure it goes without saying that the spotlight also comes with burdens. Two of the most common are being misunderstood and misrepresented. These are experiences that many face, even outside of fame. Cam was no exception to that. The media painted him as a cocky jock or a wild partier, but that wasn't my experience with him. He was a great teammate. He was kind and unselfish. He liked to laugh and cut up as much as anybody else, but in the right amount. To this day, he's one of my favorite guys to be around.

Cam, like me, surprised people when they met him in person. When you're in the public eye, people are going to form opinions. My rule is that you shouldn't hold too heavily to your preconceptions about someone until you get the chance to meet them for yourself. I have come to find that it rarely fails me. After all, we are human. Underneath the facade in a modern world, I believe that most of us are good people. Sometimes ones who have experienced a little more hurt than others, but good nonetheless.

. . .

Things were teed up nicely in Carolina. I liked the team. I had a lot of respect for head coach Ron Rivera, and it was good to be working again with offensive line coach John Matsko. I respected his approach to the game. He had a long history in the league, starting out with the Cardinals back in 1992, and coaching everywhere from the Giants to the Saints, to the Rams and Chiefs. Coach Matsko knew how to talk to me. He knew how to challenge and encourage me at the same time.

"I'm here to tell you that you're just the guy for the job," he told me in training one day. "The situation might seem impossible, but you were chosen for it."

Under these conditions, my 2015 season in Carolina was one of my best. I played in 98.4 percent of the team's snaps, allowed a career-low four sacks, and was penalized only three times for a total of twenty-five yards.

Things had been going our way that year. The 2015 season was the best single-season turnaround in the history of the Panthers. (In 2014, they'd gone 7-8-1.) We almost went undefeated, but the Falcons took us down in a Week 16 rematch at the Georgia Dome.

Still, our 2015 season was impressive by anyone's measure. We became one of only seven teams to win fifteen regular season games since the NFL expanded the schedule to sixteen in 1978. Among them, the 1984 San Francisco 49ers, the 1985 Chicago Bears (Coach Rivera's old team), the 1998 Minnesota Vikings, the 2004 Pittsburgh Steelers, the 2007 New England Patriots, and the 2011 Green Bay Packers. To be included on that list was itself a victory.

We beat the Seahawks in the divisional championship without a hitch. That win felt good for the team, since Seattle had eliminated the Panthers the year before. We went on to crush the Cardinals in the NFC Championship, 49–15. In short, everything had fallen our way all season, so we felt good going into the Super Bowl.

We should have been more skeptical.

· · ·

In February 2016, just a year after I'd been released from Tennessee, I was headed back to the Super Bowl. We were taking on the Denver Broncos in Super Bowl 50. A historic event, not just for me but for the game, which was officially having its half-century birthday. A second appearance in the Super Bowl in my short career felt like an embarrassment of riches. *Two Super Bowls in seven seasons!*

The game was held in Santa Clara, California, at Levi's Stadium, home of the San Francisco 49ers. It was the same game just three years later, but I was surprised how different this second Super Bowl felt. There was more of everything. More media. More distractions. It was a circus. Since it was the Super Bowl's golden anniversary, they took that to the max. Gold fifty-yard line. Gold gear. All-gold everything.

It was the Panthers' second Super Bowl appearance in franchise history. We had arguably the best offense in the league, despite some folks saying we were lacking in wide receivers. Cam Newton, named the NFL's MVP, was on fire. Our team wasn't facing a lot of injuries. We'd lost Kelvin Benjamin in the preseason to a torn ACL, but for the most part, we'd stayed healthy. Thomas Davis Sr., an eleven-year veteran and key linebacker for us, broke his arm in the NFC Championship. Talk about a player who wasn't going to quit! In his career, Davis had already come back from three ACL tears (something that, to my knowledge, no one else in the history of athletics has done). He swore he'd find a way to play in the Super Bowl, and sure enough, he didn't just play, he started in the game.

But despite all the odds in our favor, it wasn't our day. The Broncos got an early lead, and for the entire game, we could never get ahead. We managed to get five sacks and force two turnovers, but the Broncos clearly dominated.

I have to hand it to Peyton Manning. The guy is the truest pro I know. Peyton is one of my all-time heroes. There are few players I look up to more in the sport, but at the time of that Super Bowl, his neck was so bad he could barely throw a ball across the locker room. Statistically speaking, he'd had his worst year since his rookie year with the Colts. I remember people making a big deal about the record-breaking thirteen-year age gap between Cam Newton and Peyton Manning. He had excelled in the sport for so long. People just have no idea the kind of toll that takes on your body. Peyton was old by anyone's standard, and yet, like a true champion, he led his team and pulled off another Super Bowl victory. He hadn't made the announcement yet, but that game would be the last one of his long and impressive career. The victory was the send-off he deserved.

Aside from the Manning victory, there was another highlight from that Super Bowl. One I get asked about a lot: *What was going on with that field?*

The field at Levi's Stadium was slick. Supposedly they had replaced it three times since the stadium had been built, but still, it was the craziest field some of us had ever played. Guys were changing out their cleats in the middle of the game. For me, coming off a toe injury, it was particularly tough. There's a video of me sliding fifteen feet while blocking outside linebacker DeMarcus Ware. It was late in the first quarter. Third down. We were somewhere around the Denver 46 when I tried, as always, to anchor my left foot. But I couldn't get any traction, so as I was blocking Ware, I slid almost to the 41. That had never happened before, and it never happened again. It set the tone for the game.

I didn't complain about the field afterward because that's just not what you do. A loss is a loss. Coach Rivera is a class-act kind of guy, so he went on record saying the field was not our problem that night. "Both teams played on the same field," he said. "As far as I'm concerned, for me to be able to blame the field and try to blame it is kind of a cop-out. The truth of the matter is we both played on the surface. The surface was outstanding. I thought everything about this week was terrific."

Still, not everyone in the media was buying it. It was hard to ignore the conditions, especially when NBC Sports is writing articles titled "Who's to Blame for Michael Oher on Ice?"

There's a running joke that everybody on the offensive side will say, "We should have won that game!" But really, I agree with Coach Rivera. The loss was on us. We had had so many things go right for us that season, but in the end, we were missing the one thing required of Super Bowl champions. In short, we didn't have that sense of urgency we needed. Some of that comes with being tested. The season had been a little too easy. History had proven that for other teams before us—we were the fifth straight team to have fifteen wins and then lose the Super Bowl.

As a competitor, I absolutely hate to lose. When I looked up at the scoreboard that day and saw 24–10, it was devastating. But I'll say this: I don't think there are any failures when you're playing in the Super Bowl. There's still that feeling inside you. *Man, I made it all the way!*

I grieved the loss, but come Monday, I was ready for the next season.

I was enjoying life in Charlotte with my family. I had enough years in the league that I knew what to expect. I kept reminding myself *that* was what truly mattered. I was getting better at my position. I felt confident about what was ahead for me in Carolina— sunshine and Sunday ball games.

6

Getting Up from a Hard Hit

In football, there are the hits you are prepared for, and then there are those you don't expect. The latter of the two are the ones that knock you on your ass. Life isn't much different. We plan our whole lives to prepare ourselves to take on the challenges we think we might face. Most of the time that preparation pays off. You make it through the challenges unscathed.

However, it is often the events we never see coming that have the ability to knock us down to our darkest days. No matter how blessed someone may be, we have all experienced one of these moments. For some of us, those experiences can be life altering.

I would have never expected that the one part of my life I had prepared for the most would also be responsible for my toughest challenge yet. Ever since I was a kid, I spent every waking moment I could learning and playing the game of football. If it took ten thousand hours to master a trade, then I would be a master of the fourth degree. I loved the sport, and I wanted to be the best I could be. That meant putting in the time to prepare for every possible scenario on the field.

...

On September 18, 2016, in a Week 2 game against the San Francisco 49ers, a scenario took place that I didn't see coming. I took a hit. A *hard* hit.

Taking a hit wasn't what was unexpected. I had taken plenty of hard hits, but this one was different. My body was on the ground, but it felt like I was floating. That's the best way I can describe it. It took me a second to come to, but then I did what I always did—I picked myself back up and got off the field. It was the beginning of the fourth quarter, and even though I played the rest of the game, I don't remember it.

It's difficult for people to understand how you can do something like that without remembering it, but when you're at that level, your body is just going through the motions. Like walking or driving a car. You act without thinking.

I'd had that floating feeling one time before, the year prior. But I played through it, and eventually it went away.

Jamarca remembers saying to me over the phone the next Monday, "When Cam fumbled and that dude cracked back on you! It was bad!"

Cam had been on fire that game. He'd lit it up, but toward the end, he fumbled the ball. When the possession changes like that, the momentum on the field changes as well. You're blocking someone and suddenly the players on the defense who you are pushing against start running toward you. That's when someone hit me from behind.

After the game, even though I didn't feel right, I brushed it off. I made a joke or two about it with the guys on the sidelines. "Dude, that was a bad hit!" They weren't trying to be insensitive. They, like me, didn't know what a big deal it was. There wasn't anything said about it by the commentators. Everybody had their eyes on the fumble. Even my wife, Tiffany, who'd watched the game closer than anyone that day, didn't realize what that one play set into motion. How it would change our lives completely.

....

My mentality was to always roll with the punches. From the out-side, I was completely fine. There were no signs to take precau-tion. My injury wasn't visible, so I did my normal routine. I took Advil and went to bed that night. I couldn't quite see the injury myself, so it was easier to brush it off and let the worker in me get back to work. Be the first one in the gym. Be on the front row watching tape. Have my pen and paper out, taking notes on my last game. Stay with the schedule. Rinse and repeat.

Underneath the invisible veil of normality would be a forming injury that would alter the course of my life forever.

• • •

On September 25, 2016, I started in the last game of my career. This time we had the Vikings coming up for Week 3.

It didn't matter who you were playing. In the NFL, every game is a big game. You are at the highest level of the sport. There are very few situations that exist that would warrant an absence. I was a professional athlete. I was being paid millions to give the fans my best each and every game. Bigger than that, my own motivation would drive me to want to play.

Personally, I was competitive. I woke up every day, no matter the circumstances, to give it my all. Every step I took, I took to become better. A better player, a better teammate, a better tackle, a better husband, a better father. Excellence was my motivator, so of course I was going to play, even though my body didn't feel right.

At first, it was mostly blurred vision. Some headaches. A feeling like I was in a fog and couldn't seem to wake up. A kind of haze that clouded my mental state. In not knowing or un-derstanding what my body or mind was truly experiencing, I figured getting back on the field would help jolt me back to normal.

I don't recall much of that matchup with the Vikings. I do know the stats weren't great.

So much of that day was lost to memory, but I do know that the whole game I felt like I was lagging. My typical quickness was gone. After that game, I shared some of my symptoms with a trainer, and I was officially diagnosed with a concussion. I'd had at least two others before, but with those there was an off game or something so there was time for my body to regroup. In short, the symptoms went away before I ever needed a diagnosis. But this time, I didn't take even a day off. I just powered through.

...

The decision was made to put me in concussion protocol, which meant that I wouldn't be practicing or playing in the games but I was still with the team. The doctors told me the first week after a concussion might be rough, but things should get better after that. I just needed to stay active. Keep pushing through the discomfort, get back out on the field, and keep taking care of myself. Mind you that this was in 2016, when the impacts of concussions beyond standard symptoms were mostly unknown.

After a few weeks, it was clear I wasn't recovering as expected. And after September 16, my life got blurry for the next year and a half.

I would learn that concussion symptoms come in four categories: physical (somatic), cognitive, emotional (affective), and sleep. Unfortunately, most of them can't really be seen. For me the symptom that caused the most disruption was sleep. After that hit, it became so hard for me to fall asleep. This health issue brought with it a new challenge I wasn't quite ready for.

There was so much of me that wanted to snap my fingers and make myself better. I wanted to get back out on that field and play. Our GM, Dave Gettleman, recognized my desire to get back healthy and even told the media that I was "working [my] fanny off" to stay in shape and on top of my game. I appreciated how he checked in on me during that time, visiting me and my family at the house. His concern felt genuine, and it made me all the more motivated to get back to work.

More than anything, though, my family was my biggest drive to make my return. I wanted to keep supporting them and making them proud. It was about more than just providing for them; I wanted to be the example I had been of persevering through difficulty.

In the past, I could endure anything you threw at me. Poverty? No problem. Homelessness and starvation? No problem. Make the dean's list in college? No problem. Play in the NFL? No problem. Win the Super Bowl? No problem. You could put any challenge in front of me, and as long as I had my mind, I had the strength to accomplish it. With a concussion, I was stripped of the one tool on which I relied so heavily, my mind.

After two months in the protocol, I was still experiencing a mental fog. I had headaches, occasional slurred speech, and compounding symptoms. When I drove, I'd almost get in car wrecks, accidentally run red lights, and felt like forty miles per hour was a hundred miles per hour. I knew it wasn't right.

...

As a man, you feel responsible for lifting the burdens of your family. Before meeting Tiffany and starting our family, I was used to putting all the burdens I faced on my own shoulders. I didn't mind. It was easy to fight for that better day when you were the only one experiencing the hardship of the battle. This time it was different. This time there was no keeping my family out of the battle. As much as I tried to save them from my burdens, it wasn't possible. If something affected my health, it was going to affect my family, too.

After months of being on the injured reserve, I became eager to find a resolution to heal both my body and my mind. It was with the suggestion of a fellow teammate that I decided to go see a concussion expert, Micky Collins, in Pennsylvania.

Collins is a famous Pittsburgh-based concussion specialist. He had worked with several pro athletes with head injuries. Willing to do whatever it would take, I immediately set up a meeting. But as I was boarding the plane, I received news that would shift everything—the Panthers had let Gettleman go as general manager. Gettleman had always stood up for players, and guys like me appreciated that.

...

With Gettleman gone, things changed fast. I had entered injured reserve on November 25, 2016. Typically, most athletes on IR are removed after two weeks. I was not. I stayed on injured reserve for the remainder of my NFL career—almost a year and a half. On July 20, 2017, the Panthers announced my release from their contract.

My head was flooded with a number of emotions and thoughts when the news of it went public. I was now facing a new climb in life. The mountaintop success of my two Super Bowl visits was over. The heights of the past were in the rearview and I was once again at a crossroads.

Since my rise out of the projects, I hadn't allowed myself to rest. Once I had made the decision to earn that better life, it was a nonstop race to the finish. Now at thirty-one years old I had crossed that finish line.

What else is there?

I am somebody who is always on the move. Like I said, my whole adult life was spent chasing greatness. Now I was still. The quiet of life was enough to give me the space to think. I was finally alone with no influence. I had nothing except my family and the situation with my health. My next decision would be critical.

This game had my heart. I put so much of myself into it. Blood, sweat, and tears. In many ways it was a part of who I was. Every situation in life comes with choices, though. Mine were simple.

Do I stay in the game or do I heal?

7

The Choice to Be Well

You are defined by your choices. It is a lesson and truth that I have clung to in life. I know from firsthand experience that the circumstances you find yourself in may not be a true reflection of who you are, but rather the choices you make when faced with those circumstances.

There are many people who would have thought my career was over the second they heard the news. That was not the case with me. Being released from the Panthers just seemed like another obstacle to face at the time. In all honesty, I wasn't ready to give up. The fighter in me wanted to get back to where I once was. I knew my body had what it took, all I had to do was put in the hard work to get it there.

My thoughts were swirling around in my head:

Eight seasons doesn't feel like enough.

I have more to give.

What if I take another hit like that? Was it worth the risk?

The tug-of-war in my mind took place because of an even greater commitment I had pulling for my decision. I had always promised myself that if I ever became a father, I was going to be there for my kids. I actually put it in writing. In my last book, I made this promise: "I'm going to be a great father, do all the right things, and make sure I'm there for them."

Could I be a real and constant presence in their lives if I continued to damage the one thing that made me, me?

As I was sitting there thinking about this one night, I heard my kids playing in the next room, and I thought to myself: *You know your answer. It's time to hang it up.*

Suddenly, the hard decision was easy.

I was going to walk away from the game I love, the game that changed my life, the game that changed me—while I still could.

...

After football, my whole life changed. My first focus would be on addressing the condition I found myself in as a result of the concussion. Before, I got up and went to the weight room for training. Now I would be starting my mornings off with about a dozen medications before going to rehab. Beyond the physical and mental health aspects, I also had my employment to think about. Technically speaking, I was jobless. I had a family I was responsible for, so figuring out my future employment was at the front of my mind.

When it came to making decisions on how to deal with the effects of my concussion, I would normally defer to the doctors. They were the experts, so I trusted their guidance. Their approach was mostly medicinal. *If this one doesn't work, then we'll drop it and up that one.*

It wasn't that I wanted to disengage from the treatment, it was just that the approach was foreign to me. Every injury is different. With the body, it's all about learning how to compensate. Behind the scenes, your mind is like a puppeteer controlling the strings. It tells whatever it is—that shoulder, that bicep, that hip—to follow the physical therapist. To trust in the process. That the way out of the pain is through it.

For the most part, these statements hold true for physical

injury. Unfortunately, none of it applies to head injuries. With a head injury, the mind can't override the situation. And for someone like me, whose secret weapon has always been mindset, this was particularly tough. All my life I have been able to use my brain to navigate tough circumstances. It was the one foolproof tool in my tool kit. Because of my positive mindset, I'd managed to get through decades of trauma on my body and spirit, but this was something entirely different.

The uncertainty of my condition was the hardest aspect to face. It was like walking out onto the field for a game without a playbook. There was no cheat sheet to tell me what to do next. I wouldn't have my team to help pull me out of this bind, either. I was facing the darkening void of my declining mental health without a guiding light.

The symptoms of my head injury clouded my experiences and perceptions like a constant haze hanging over my head. It was a weird feeling to experience, but it felt as if I wasn't myself. It was like watching something else take over and go through the motions of my life. That was a difficult experience for me. I care deeply about making other people happy, but I couldn't do that in my current state. As a result, I decided to remove myself from the scenario. I couldn't stand the thought of bringing everyone down. Of course, those who knew me best tried to help in the ways they could. Tiffany and Jamarca would take turns trying to get me out of the house, but it was hard to leave the comfort and darkness of my room.

...

I knew that I had to find my way out of that bedroom, but when I finally did so two years later, I weighed 430 pounds.

The weight gain was strange. Anyone who knows me knows I keep to my diet like clockwork. I eat green even on the weekends.

I don't eat barbecue unless it's a special occasion; instead I've got twelve recipes for cod.

In the past, it didn't matter what trials I had faced. My internal motivation always seemed to be full and ready to spend. This time, it felt as if all that motivation had been drained. I was running on empty. It felt impossible to go to the kitchen and make a smoothie when it was hard to even stand up straight.

My weight spiked quickly, even though many days I was too sick to really get out of bed. Before I knew it, I went from 310 to about 370, seemingly overnight. In reality it was about a three-month transformation. Light in general was also difficult, so I'd stay in my room with the curtains drawn. Tiffany would leave food at the door when she started to worry. I wanted to explain to her what was going on, but even I couldn't explain it. I knew people loved me and wanted to help, but they couldn't get it. I just didn't have the energy to engage anymore. I even pulled off of Instagram and other social media.

It was a slow, paralyzed sink into one of my darkest times. For me, the lowest moment came in the spring of 2017. I was flying back and forth to Pittsburgh to get shots in the back of my neck for migraines. On one of these flights, I reached for my seat belt for takeoff, but it wouldn't fasten. I looked around, feeling awkward. I tried again, but the two metal clasps weren't even close. I didn't know if they were going to kick me off the plane or not, so I tried to hide it. I put a magazine in my lap, but the flight attendant had eyes like a hawk. "You need to buckle up, sir." But then she realized I couldn't. She went down the aisle and came back with something called a seat belt extender—a thing I didn't even know existed. I took it from her, and she smiled like it was no big deal. But I was humiliated.

On the plane ride, I sat there in silence. *You've got everything you ever wanted—your family, your kids, your own home. But without your health, you've got nothing. You can't enjoy the fruits of your labor. Your whole life should be ahead of you, but it's basically coming to an end right now.*

When I got home, I knew what I had to do. The needle that had rested on *E* for so long was creeping back up. The fighter in me was returning.

The orange Rx bottles were all lined up on the counter, waiting for me when I walked in. Without hesitation, I scooped them up and, instead of opening them, I threw them in the trash—all of them.

Don't get me wrong, I'm an advocate for science, but I gave the experts their time. Deep down I knew the prescriptions weren't serving me. In reality they were a patch, tools that helped numb the pain between doses. I wanted to take control.

That was the turning point. In my darkest season at my lowest moment, I stepped up and said, "Enough." When everything seemed to be crashing in on me, I took action on the decision to be better. This time it wasn't about escaping the projects or poverty. This time it was about being healthy. I was going to fight to regain my strength, my mind. To do so, I was going to have to start by healing my body first. Even before I had time to make any progress, I felt lifted. It was like I opened my eyes for the first time. The darkness surrounding me didn't seem so dark after all. There was hope. I had a chance to be well again.

• • •

I remember the first day. It was a combination of nerves as I got in my car and drove to the park in my neighborhood called Granny White. At this point, it had been months since I'd even driven a car.

I sat in my truck for a minute and stared out the windshield. It was midday, midweek, so it was mostly mothers and strollers.

Will anyone be able to recognize me? I thought as I climbed out. It was early summer in Tennessee, so it was hot. Really hot. But in my mind, the plan was already in motion. I had a choice to make—and I chose to be well. There was no going back on it.

As I took the first few steps across the parking lot, I was a little in shock at how far I was from where I'd been. A year and a half before, I had run out onto the field for the Super Bowl. I had not only played, but started in the mecca of sporting events. And there I was, panting in an empty parking lot, nervous about a walk in a park.

See the basketball court. Make it to there, I coached myself.

I couldn't have been more than a quarter of a football field away, but the way I was exerting myself, you would have thought I was back at two-a-days in Mississippi.

You take everything I've ever been through in my life. All those tough breaks as a kid that made me "famous"—the weight of hunger and poverty, the betrayal of people who called themselves family, the failures of the foster care system they put me in—all of it was a cakewalk compared to where I was in that moment.

But I knew I still had that engine deep down inside me, and I could access it if I tried.

I could only power walk about fifteen feet before I was so exhausted I had to stop. I caught my breath and went again. Another few feet, another break. I caught my breath.

Rinse and repeat, until I reached the park's basketball court. I caught my breath. I stared up at the reinforced rims on the hoop. Granny White was in the Nashville neighborhood of Brentwood. Those tax dollars meant nice facilities at the park, right down to the hoops. At that moment, I wished more than anything I had the energy to run around the court again. Or even to take one good shot.

I'll be back.

I didn't know when, but I knew I'd be healthy enough to play again. I turned and started the walk back to my truck. It was the shortest workout of my entire life, but somehow I left there feeling satisfied. I had done the hardest thing. *Once it's down to 364, it's on,* I told myself. I got the first day out of the way. The momentum of direction in my life had changed course. This time I was on the right track.

• • •

Persistence pays off. That was a lesson I knew even as a little boy. Now it was time to make those investments of hard work and sacrifice again. A few more days went by, and I was still doing my thing. Showing up. Walking it out. Working up a sweat.

I had plans for the future. Big plans. Like I had as a kid from Hurt Village, I envisioned myself past the situation. I saw where I wanted to be, not tomorrow but a hundred tomorrows away. The master plan is important, no doubt, but like Pastor Dale says, "Sufficient is the trouble for the day." What that meant to me is that I was going to put the big goals on the shelf. I would tackle the challenge right in front of me. I knew where I wanted to be, but for now it had to be about that next step.

I showed up each day at Granny White like I was back at the Under Armour Performance Center with the Ravens. It was serious to me, and even though no one was there to see it, I wasn't going to miss a day of workouts.

No surprise I got some stares. It comes with the territory of fame. Beyond that was my size and color. It's not every day you see a big Black man barreling down a walking path at lunchtime on a Tuesday in Brentwood, Tennessee. For me, it was nothing new. I shrugged off the stares, as I had back at Briarcrest.

But one afternoon, there was a particular stranger who seemed to keep staring at me. It wasn't a normal stare, like when someone is sizing you up or something. I can't really explain it except that I felt like he was a good dude.

Still, I was in no talking mood. Especially not during my training, so I tucked my head down every time he nodded at me on the walking path. I could tell by the way the guy carried himself that he was also an athlete. He had some high school kids jogging ahead and behind him, so I assumed he was a coach, probably at Brentwood High School.

The last time he passed, I saw he was looking at the Ravens logo on my shorts, so I assumed maybe he'd figured out who I was, and at that point in my life, I was in no mood to chitchat with strangers about the good old days, so I thought I'd make one more lap and head back.

But when I got there, he was standing by my truck, waiting for me.

"Are you Michael Oher?" he asked across the parking lot.

"*Lord Jesus*," I muttered to myself, trying to prepare to be patient.

I nodded yes. And then I couldn't help myself, so I added, "Don't believe everything you read." After my release from the NFL, my name had been in the news and not for reasons that I wanted. So naturally, I was on the defensive.

He smiled uncomfortably. "Not sure what exactly you're talking about. I don't read much news anyway."

I kind of furrowed my eyebrows at him.

"Really, dude, I don't know what you're talking about. Definitely no judgment." The way he was looking at me, I believed him.

We talked for a minute, and then he said the strangest thing. "Michael, do you mind if . . ." He hesitated.

At that time, when someone started a question with the phrase

"Do you mind?" my whole body would tense. Not because I didn't want to help, but because I was so drained, so depleted. I felt like I had nothing I could give. For so long, the "Do you mind?" question was followed with a request. A picture, an autograph, a statement to the press.

But this stranger wanted nothing from me. He actually had something to give.

"God told me to pray for you," he said. "Do you mind if I do that?"

I'll admit, it's way less awkward if someone just asks for an autograph. It was a little weird, but also comforting. My life had taken a turn for the better. I was on my journey to healing, but I was still a long way from a good place. I wasn't really turning away prayers, even if they came from someone I'd just met.

"Sure," I said. "Go ahead." I bowed my head as he laid a hand on my shoulder.

His prayer for me wasn't anything fancy or flowery. I didn't feel the ground shake. But I remember the final line of the prayer. I hadn't heard anything that powerful in a long time: "Whatever direction he is going, I ask you, God, lift his spirit."

I thought it was amazing. This man had no idea the emotional weight I was carrying, and yet he was reading what was on my heart and praying for me.

I lifted my head. I was still the same sweaty, overweight guy, but I felt different. I felt lighter somehow. Without knowing it, this stranger became someone I had been subconsciously looking for. Someone to validate my pain. A hand in the darkness. Even if it was just for that moment, I didn't have to shoulder my burdens alone.

I believe that is how life was designed to be. We are supposed to face our challenges and burdens together. Reality, however, oftentimes plays out in stark contrast. I was grateful for the moment

I didn't have to face my troubles alone, because for so much of my life that is what I had done. As a kid, finding my way through a problem or situation was a solo performance. Having that expectation prepared me for many challenges in life; in particular, my survival on the streets. That is why I will always be an advocate for promoting one's ability to persevere alone. For many, it is necessary for survival. But that doesn't mean it has to be the only solution. I admire those who find themselves in a season of strength, who use it as an opportunity to help those in their moments of need. It is a defining trait of humanity that I love—our willingness to love others in their darkest hour.

...

Tangled up in my recovery is one simple concept and I'm afraid it's lost on today's generation: patience.

I kept up my routine. All it took was for me to see the number on the bathroom scale go down one time and I was locked in. What made the weight loss process even more satisfying was the ownership I got to take in it. For once, I was doing something that someone wasn't going to pop up and take the credit for.

I've always been a big guy. Sticking to a diet, even losing some weight, is something I've long been familiar with, but this time was very different. It wasn't just that I needed to shed a few pounds to help me run faster or make weigh-in. This was a life-or-death kind of different. On Sundays, I'd been about 310—and more of it was muscle back then. I was a hundred-plus pounds from a healthy weight. To see that first number on the bathroom scale go down not once, but twice, was going to take time. There was something Coach Matsko had said to me during a training session that suddenly came back to me: *Stack good days on top of good days.*

So that became my mantra. Just one good day after the next.

I knew that if I could just lose a pound a day, those pounds would start to add up. This was a game plan I could understand. It went all the way back to my roots: If I could go to that one class. If I could do that one rep. If I could make it through the night to the next morning. If these single actions could stack up, over time, I could really have something to work with. Victory is won in inches.

That's the thing: you gotta be willing to put in the time, even if the desired result isn't within sight. That's my fear these days. Kids are being raised on fifteen-second TikTok videos. Their minds don't know how to wait. How to dig deep for the fortitude to play the long game. And now, as I'm looking back on it, as I'm thinking about how to advise my own son, I can see that situation even more clearly. The driving factor in all of it for me is a quality that, in today's world, is going the way of the dinosaurs.

Patience.

That fruit you planted is going to grow, but what it requires is months and months of staring at dirt.

...

When you find the light, you escape the dark. My journey out of my darkest season took the better part of three years to complete. In a way, it was the longest game I ever had to play. Except this time, instead of winning the Lombardi Trophy, I won my life back. It was the sweetest victory I ever claimed.

As the light began to flood back into my life, it would bring with it new horizons. My journey wasn't over. A new chapter had just begun. This one would be the brightest yet.

8

New Horizons

Tomorrow carried a purpose beyond me. That was the thought racing through my head as I stepped outside of the pristine building on Vanderbilt's campus, where the Wond'ry was located. It was the first of what would be many meetings and visits on that campus. It was there that my vision for this new direction in life would take form. For once, I was directing the story being told. For once, I had a say in what I wanted my life to be about. For once I could think about the legacy I would be leaving behind and find peace. This time, it wouldn't be about Michael Oher. This time it would be bigger than just me.

Before I can share any of the details about what was built at Vanderbilt, I must first take you all the way back to that seven-year-old boy who made the stories you have heard possible. And yes, for this moment, I am talking about me.

Before the fame, before the football, and even before the education, there was only a little boy experiencing life within the walls of a few blocks of the Memphis projects. From the outside you might not have found anything special about me or my life, but you couldn't tell me that. To me, I was special. I don't know where I even learned to think like that. As a kid who had nothing else to grab on to, I grabbed on to the idea that I was important. There wasn't anyone else who was Michael Oher. It didn't matter what my circumstances were, I was special and nothing was going to take that away from me.

In that one thought, I would give my mind the strength it needed to cultivate the characteristics of someone who could earn success. When you believe something strongly enough, you will begin to will it into existence. A runner who believes they are a champion practices every day. An artist who believes they are talented will push the boundaries of their brush. A chess player who believes they are the best challenges the smartest opponents. For me, I believed I could make it. I believed that I could earn a life free from pain and anguish. So, in a life of seeming hopelessness, I looked for opportunity.

. . .

In those early days opportunity was rare. Even as a child, I understood and knew that my options would be limited. When you are facing that kind of a realization, you can have one of two reactions. Either you can see the negative and let your mind turn you into a victim, or you can see the positive and be thankful that an opportunity could exist. I myself chose the latter. By doing so, I would ensure that I wouldn't let the chance at a better life pass me by. I was going to be prepared the only way I knew how.

I looked to my hero for inspiration, Michael Jordan. What he embodied was the principle to always do what was right. I woke up every single day making that decision to do the same. I steered clear of violence. I didn't touch drugs. I woke up early. I worked hard at everything. I didn't take shortcuts. By doing this day in and day out, I built a foundation for myself. That foundation was my character. I was defining the person I was going to be. That person would be a hard worker, an honest person, and someone who could persevere through adversity. When you build that kind of foundation, you put yourself in a position to take advantage of the opportunities you find in life.

My early life had many walls—homelessness, starvation, poverty. If I couldn't find my window of opportunity in the moment, I would simply look farther down the road. By the time I reached the ninth grade, not much looked different in my life. Apart from my character, I was still experiencing many of the hardships I've shared with you previously. To me, my window of escape was education. I thought to myself:

If I can just make it into some junior college, even a community college, that is all I need.

I knew that was all I needed in order to ensure my success. I was determined to find my way in life. It didn't matter what you threw at me, I was going to find a way to twist it to my advantage.

...

My life became a wellspring of blessings. Beyond the odds and the walls was a life better than I could have ever dreamed of. Not only did I become an NFL player, but I played among the best. I had made enough to never worry about another meal again. I had a healthy family who loved me and a good house in a safe neighborhood. I had everything little Mike could have ever wanted. If I had been anyone else, that endless race for personal prosperity would have been over right there. After recovering from my concussion, I could have lay low with relatively little to no worry in life. The race was over. It was time to rest. *Right?*

As comforting as it might have been to rest, I knew that it wasn't over. There was that urge in the back of my head pushing me to do something more. I set in my mind to chase greatness at the age of seven. I wired every fiber of my being to operate and become better with each passing day. The difference between then and now was life. My experiences through the years brought wisdom. I learned that becoming great had more to do with what you did for others than what you did for yourself. In knowing that, I couldn't quit.

That chase for greatness would be an everlasting race to participate in the greater good with my fellow humans. All of a sudden, I would understand what it meant to be special. You see, being special didn't mean that I was more important. I never thought that. Being special means that you have a purpose that is unique to you.

Just like every part of a body has purpose, so does each of us have a purpose in building our community. The heart pumps the blood, the lungs fill it with oxygen, and the stomach provides nutrition. Each one is different from the last, but they all work together with their own purpose to support the body they are all a part of. If one of those parts isn't working as it should, then the whole body suffers. Humanity is no different. We as a community are the body, and the individuals that make it up are like the parts of the body. If even one of us doesn't work to our purpose, then the community at large is what suffers.

As a kid I was facing circumstances that were bound to ensure that I didn't live to fulfill my purpose. Bad fortune was like a disease trying to kill the potential I had. I wasn't going to take it lying down. I knew there was a reason to my existence. I wasn't a mistake. I would fight for my opportunity to be useful, to give back. After thirty-two years, I would be coming face-to-face with that opportunity I had worked so hard for.

· · ·

Compassion revealed my second purpose. I often hear otherwise. Leaders give the advice "Do what you are passionate about."

That is advice I can agree with, but I feel like it can be taken even further.

No human is an island. Everything we do affects someone else. So if each of us has a reason for being here, we must conclude that our purpose lies within our ability to help others in some form or capacity.

My passion was football for so long. It was the sport I loved and still love. I got to play it and give back the gift of entertainment for others. But that chapter of my life was now closed. If I was going to continue to live with meaning, I would have to seek out another passion. At first that was difficult.

How can I pivot after a life of preparing myself for a world so unique as professional sports?

My answer would come to me in the same place I started this story with you, all the way back at Big Oak Ranch.

Seeing a former NFL star like Brodie Croyle find a revived mission in life outside of football was educational, but it wasn't the reason for my awakening. Instead, it was witnessing kids like me have an opportunity at living their life to its fullest. My time with those kids at the ranch was more than just a visit down memory lane. In that night spent there, I witnessed kids who faced some of the same exact traumas I had faced as a child get to have fun. It was like for those moments the weight of their burdens was lifted.

My heart beat intensely thinking about each of their lives. I was thankful that they had a place like Big Oak Ranch where they would be cared for and given the resources needed to thrive. After I left, my feelings for those kids would remain. They would grow more and more to encompass all the kids who I knew were experiencing the hurt and turmoil of broken homes and poverty. What I began to realize was that my passion for a game was being replaced by a new kind of passion. This passion was born from the compassion for kids like me.

I wanted to help kids who had everything going against them in life. I wanted to ensure they had an opportunity to find their purpose. There was one aspect that I did want to be different. Unlike me, I wanted them to be able to have fun while chasing greatness. What I mean by that is, I wanted them to be able to be kids. I didn't want to just reach my hand out with a check and say, "Here you go, here's your chance." I wanted to be a part of lifting their burdens so that they had an opportunity to enjoy the process of finding their own passion and pursuing it. They shouldn't have to bear the burden of survival as they chased who they were meant to be.

My compassion for those kids and others like them gave me my new direction in life. I was excited and ready to attack my hopes and dreams like the first Sunday game of a season. There was only one problem. I didn't have a plan or clue about how I could exactly help these kids. Before you can play a game, you must first have a playbook. That is where I would start in this new season of life.

...

Knowledge is the real currency of the world. If you have it, you have the power to shape your life the way you want it.

As I think back on my own life, knowledge was the first step on my rise out of poverty. Securing a good education was the first opportunity I seized as a kid. Everything else in my life, blessings and accomplishments, flowed from there. Without education I wouldn't have had football, my family, or the platform I have today. Knowledge has the ability to open any door you want in life.

So when I thought of ways to equip these kids to escape the

cycles of poverty and hopelessness, I thought of education. Education is the resource of securing knowledge. It equips kids to be prepared for life. If they have it, then they have the tools to succeed.

Providing education for the youth of America would seem like it should be a relatively easy affair. After all, education is nothing more than organized information.

How hard could it be to share information?

The answer, as I would come to find out, would be "very hard."

After leaving my first meeting with Pastor Dale, I was excited to tackle the challenges ahead. Those forewarned obstacles I would face were nothing but more walls for me to hurdle. As fun as it was to play in the NFL, game day had nothing on giving back to people in a more purposeful way. The months ahead would attest that I would need the energy that came with my passion for educating youth.

I had board meeting after board meeting. I met with counselors, teachers, boards of education, and even governors. Month after month passed as I put my nose to the grindstone and dipped into my wallet day after day to ensure my dream could be a reality.

My first year and attempt would lead to a dead end. Legal restrictions and red tape surrounding the heavily regulated education system would deter my first approach at providing education to disadvantaged youth. That wall wouldn't stop me, though. I am not a quitter. To me there is no such thing as failure, only lessons learned. So I decided to begin again. I wasn't ready to give up.

. . .

Pursuing objectives of virtue strengthens your ability to persevere. Providing access to better education was paramount. It was a key ingredient to my own success story. My life was a testament to education's capabilities. You could say I was a firm believer in the solution I was dedicated to providing.

As I was readying myself to take another hard swing at starting a program for kids surrounding education, I would be reconnected with some old family friends of mine from my days at Briarcrest. It was around the summer of 2019 when I would approach the Sparks for guidance on my foundation. I had originally offered them a seat on the board.

The Sparks were one of the families who had extended their help to me at Briarcrest. They had a son in my class, Justin. In many ways they were like a mother and father to me. I can honestly say that the love and care I received from them as a kid was one of the few experiences of genuine heartfelt assistance that I received after Tony entered my life. It is a big reason why I approached them. I knew I could depend on their honest and goodhearted nature to guide me through the process. There's a lesson in that. Knowing not only when but also who to approach for wise council can have the biggest impact on your outcome.

Choosing to partner with the Sparks Foundation would turn out to be the right decision. Beyond their ability of entrepreneurship, they were also well connected to the individuals I would need in order to move beyond the obstacles I had faced in my first attempt. They would introduce me to a gentleman at Vanderbilt by the name of Stryker Warren.

Everything about Stryker commanded a strong impression. Apart from a name fit for a general, his appearance, posture, demeanor, and lexicon constituted traits of a resolved and learned leader. It was without surprise that I heard of the long list of accolades he had accrued prior to taking up a position at Vanderbilt University. It was during my first meeting with him that I knew he had what it would take to bring my vision to life. After I'd shared my goals with him, he would open up the plethora of facilities and programs that Vanderbilt University had to offer.

Programs like the Wond'ry, an innovation center that provides incubators for start-ups and entrepreneurs, were the exact resource I needed to take my foundation to the next level. In those programs I would meet Deanna Meador, the director of entrepreneurship. Between the efforts of both Stryker and Deanna, I would be surrounded by the best players in the game. In just six months, I would have a team of dedicated individuals who would go on to form a real, viable approach to improve the opportunities for education for disadvantaged youth.

The key to it all would be re-creating the aspects of my story that made my life a success. My desire and dream is to have my story be commonplace. My life shouldn't be a miracle. Kids who dream to succeed and are willing to put in the hard work to earn that life for themselves should have the opportunity to pursue their passions. Circumstances of poverty, homelessness, or parental instability should not be limiting factors that prohibit our kids, our future, from achieving their potential.

(What would culminate from my compassion for kids with a hunger to learn would be the Oher Foundation. If you find yourself equally passionate about my initiative, please look online and reach out to learn about the ways you can get involved and join me on my mission.)

...

New horizons carried the promise of a better tomorrow. I am now beginning a new journey in my life. This newfound mission is one that I hope will survive beyond me. I am ready to ride out the objective through all seasons to come so that no child will have to face what I faced, but may reap what we sow together.

Even in prosperity, I faced walls in the later seasons of my life.

It is an unavoidable truth that is inescapable even in success. That is why I chose to write this second book. Beyond where I see my future in the education of youth, I see and understand the value of my experiences. I hope that my stories strike a common thread with the people who read them. I believe that you as a reader will find similarities even with your own life.

More than anything I want to help those who are experiencing their own walls in life. If you are in a season of defeat, hardship, pain, adversity, or challenge, please stay with me. I would like to share the lessons I learned when I faced those dark seasons of my life when my back was against a wall. Know that you don't have to stay there. There is a way out.

What follows is my playbook on life and how I found my way out of and beyond the walls I was facing from childhood to now. My wish is that it will guide you to that better season, where opportunities of healing and progress await.

PART II
The Playbook

9

#1: It Starts with Want-To

Want-to is a lifeboat. It's not something that can be bought, or even taught.

When I think back on my life, want-to was the driving force. It was what got me over one hurdle . . . and then the next.

There's a saying that I often share with groups: There is no such thing as a morning person. That person doesn't exist. The "morning people" are the people who went to bed early so they could get up the next day. I *wanted* to go to school, so I bought my own alarm clock. If I hadn't done that, I would have missed the bus.

I *wanted* to have food in the fridge, so I got a job selling newspapers.

I *wanted* to be the best offensive lineman I could be, so I studied YouTube videos of Orlando Pace and applied what I saw to my own technique.

Want-to requires effort, and you can't teach effort. It's like a natural resource. It comes from inside you, and you tap into it— or not.

When I was ten or eleven, the foster system was done with me. Maybe my file got lost in the shuffle or they were just tired of trying to find me. Like a boat untied from the dock, they let me drift. That could have been the end of Michael Oher. I could have settled for the status quo. I looked around. Nobody in my community had a high school degree. Nobody had a job. Nobody *wanted* a job. I don't say that to be critical. It's hard to break the cycle if you don't know another way exists. It's not that they weren't capable. It's not even that they didn't have the resources. You can get the resources. Most of the time, if you are persistent, you can find a way out of a bad situation. The ultimate problem in my community was that many didn't want more for themselves. For many (maybe even the majority), they didn't know to want more.

Want-to is the common denominator for change and for success—and I'm not just talking athletes. You cannot overcome an obstacle unless you *want* to. That's the key in the ignition. I would still be in my bedroom today if I hadn't had that aha moment with my seat belt on that plane ride. I had to reach the point where I couldn't take any more. Where I said, *Enough.*

Think about a tough situation in your life: Do you truly *want* to change it?

If you do, then guess what? You have the power of want-to. It's also all you need to get started.

. . .

Want-to takes different shapes. It's in your attitude, but it's also in your appearance.

For me, that means looking like I care. Looks matter because they say something about you. They can say you have prepared. You have taken care of your body and mind. That you respect yourself. Even if you don't have a lot of money to spend on your wardrobe, you can be neat. You can comb your hair and wash your face. There was a long period in my life when if I had only one hole in my shirt, I felt like I was doing good. Even with the hole right there in the middle of my chest, I made sure that shirt was clean and pressed and I held my head up. Deion Sanders said something I always share: "If you look good, you feel good. . . . If you feel good, you play good, if you play good, they pay good."

Looks matter. Not for vanity's sake, but for results.

This principle is something I want to implement with my foundation: *Look like you want to be here.* Maybe that means button-up shirts, bow ties, flat khakis. We want to teach boys and girls early on that want-to can be communicated through how you present yourself. You can express yourself through how you dress, but you must convey to others that you took the time to care.

Want-to also comes out in your preparation. The early bird gets the worm, but it's more than that. Don't just be an early bird—there are a lot of those out there. Be the earliest bird.

It's a simple analogy, but I think about this every morning when I'm taking my son to school. I try to get out of my neighborhood, but when I pull down the drive to turn onto the main road, there's already traffic.

That tells me one thing: showing up on time and leaving on time is for the average guy. If you want to excel, you gotta do better than that. Nowadays, when I have to be somewhere, I show up thirty minutes early. If I have a meeting and I'm not waiting on the other person to get there, I consider myself late.

Want-to is in your posture. Sometimes in sports, the secret is positioning. A slight shift of your body this way or that, and suddenly you have an edge. This trick didn't come to me in the NFL. It didn't come to me in college. It came to me in Hurt Village. As a kid I knew that enthusiasm was a way I could tap into energy. So, in the mornings, I didn't just get out of bed—I jumped.

Want-to in my body language was extremely helpful in my education. My first year at Briarcrest, going from class to class was like running one mental obstacle course after the next. I wasn't used to that pace. But as I learned back then, your posture speaks volumes. When I was working on a class project, even if I wasn't the person leading my group, I made sure my body language was right. I sat up straight. I had my book open. I was energized, and because of that, I sometimes found the answers I wouldn't have if I'd been sitting there with a bad attitude.

• • •

Football is the ultimate want-to sport. Not taking anything away from basketball, because I absolutely loved it. In basketball, like in football, you've got to mentally prepare for the battle on the court, but you have one thing in your favor—the arena. What do I mean by that?

Two words: climate control. Basketball players don't have to deal with the elements. No record-breaking heat. No snow and rain. You're not putting on cleats when it's subzero outside.

Back at Ole Miss, an offensive line coach took notice of my want-to. He said once in front of the other guys, "It starts sprinkling outside and you all are ready to hang it up. But Mike's always running out onto the field, ready to go."

I didn't like being singled out, but it was true. When you have want-to, it will override the average guy's excuse.

In the NFL, my want-to went to another level. It had to. As I've said, even as a first-rounder, I went into the Ravens facility that first day like I was going to get cut.

I knew I had to position myself to win, and the best way to do that was repetition. You see, your mind won't tell your body to do something it hasn't already been doing. You can try, but your body is gonna be like: *We haven't been working on this!*

This applies to anything from football to parenting. Start putting in now and I promise at some point you'll see dividends. Whether it is a sport or a relationship, you get out what you put in.

And for the young people, time is on your side. Don't waste it. Think of it like a long-term investment, a Roth IRA. You can put in a little bit every day. You have the time, so use it wisely. Make every day count toward your future goals.

In football—or in any sport—there are countless examples of this. For an offensive tackle, whatever side of the ball you're playing on, you want your inside leg to be as strong as possible. So, in training, I would get on one leg (like a shot-putter) and do set after set until my inside leg got extremely explosive. I haven't played football in years, but when I go to the gym nowadays, I can still feel the difference between my strong and weak legs. It's muscle memory. It's part of our genetic makeup. The brain is hardwired to create shortcuts. Like the best Apple product, it can predict the things you do and say all the time. The synapses in your brain reinforce what is habit.

After I was released from the NFL, after I had gone through my darkest days and was on the path to getting healthy again, I knew that my want-to would require me to make some choices. I only had so much bandwidth mentally and physically, so that meant I would have to say no to good things. I'd have to sacrifice certain activities, even certain relationships. Sometimes you have to narrow your field of view so that you can focus on what you really want. At that time, I wanted one thing: to get healthy for my family.

My repetition became my daily routine. For many personality types, *routine* is a dirty word. Routines can be boring. Truthfully, they're almost always boring. We want new. We want exciting. There's nothing glorious about the day in, day out.

That was very clear when my friend visited me from Florida recently. You might think this is crazy, but even though he was in town, I kept to my workout routine. It's a simple regimen, but it involves the sauna, weights, and cardio, and when I am in a phase of getting healthy, my workout is as nonnegotiable for me as food and sleep.

My friend knows this about me. He's been in my life for over a decade. He's seen me at my worst and at my best (which I hope is right at this moment). He knows that when I'm in the zone, when I've committed to a plan, there are few things that can make me deviate from it. Anyone who knows the hardship I've been through these past few years also knows that this health journey for me is sort of sacred.

So I stay the course. These days, instead of a million-dollar NFL facility, I work out in my home gym. I have a simple but effective Legend Fitness machine in my garage, and that's where I go in the mornings. The kids are in school, so it's usually quiet. Training has always been one of the most solitary things I do. I get completely lost in my head, and it's a beautiful thing.

Because I take my workout process so seriously, I'm funny about trainers. In fact, it's safe to say I regress every time I hire one. I know my body by now. I've been through this enough. Again, it goes back to want-to. If you have want-to, you aren't going to put matters into the hands of someone who doesn't know you. You take matters into your own hands. Trainers don't get my desire. They don't understand that I can't be rushed. They have their clients lined up, so what does that mean for me? It means fifty-seven minutes of sweat, and they're gone within an hour. But I'm barely warmed up. I'm all about not rushing what's important.

I work out my hamstrings with resistance bands. I jump rope. I ride a few miles on my stationary bike. Most days, I toss a weight ball against the stone wall outside my garage. Shoulders, core—it's working a lot of things at one time. It's a humble routine, but sometimes that's all it takes.

I usually try to incorporate some hoops, so I met a buddy at

Granny White Park. He fed me the ball as I shot around the perimeter.

"This is what it takes to be a champion?" he asked.

"One hundred percent." I laughed. "The slow grind is the secret."

We were joking, but I believe it. It's the little things that count.

And let's bring it all the way back to the beginning: Without want-to, you won't do those little things. It won't matter enough. You'll check out when the days get hard. You make small concessions—*No big deal if I skip a workout today. I'll get up earlier tomorrow. I'll work on my résumé next week.* Whatever the excuse is, it'll keep you from having the momentum you need to change your situation.

· · ·

If routine and repetition are crucial, the reverse is also true: you cannot succeed without them.

This is why I was particularly frustrated every time I got the marching orders that I was changing positions again. Relocating from left tackle to right tackle, and then a season later, switching back again. What I wanted more than anything was to stay put so I would have a long enough runway to get my technique just perfect. I'm a perfectionist, and perfectionists like repetition. I believe in it because I'm a believer in the process. I'm a fan of good foundation and good technique. Those who are truly great at anything do not take shortcuts.

Nowadays, the NFL seems to be more thoughtful about this when they draft players. They acknowledge it more and more in the way they approach positions. They don't switch guys— particularly offensive tackles—like they did with me. Like I said earlier, it's a very big change. Right and left tackle may have the same footwork, but it's with opposite legs. The best comparison is this: Whatever hand you write with, try to write with the other hand. Then try to take a timed test with that nondominant hand. Then try to take that test with an All-Pro defensive end or pass rusher bearing down on you.

You see what I'm saying? Part of it is in your mind: You lose a mental edge when something is new. It feels unfamiliar, so your head game is off. But the other part is that muscle memory.

For better or worse, I forced myself to make the transition every time I was asked. I acted like it was no big deal, so the coaches were always more inclined to move me. As I said, I realize now that that was a consequence of being a team player. I say I would do things differently if I went back today, but I don't know if I would. I cannot separate my want-to from what's best for the team. But this is one of the many areas where I think the game has gotten better since I left. Coaches and coordinators have started to acknowledge the power of repetition.

The moral of the story is that without repetition, it's hard to master anything. And without want-to, you will not be willing to put in those reps. You will be bored; you will make excuses. Dedication and daily sweat are the only keys to long-term success. Sure, there are those flash-in-the-pan moments of talent or genius, but for lasting accomplishments, you've got to be consistent. For those in the back, let me say it again: consistency (repetition) is essential in anything you want to achieve.

When your back's against the wall, the very first thing you need is want-to. Want-to is your ignition, but it's also your engine. Certain seasons of life are going to test your want-to. Hardship will test it. But want-to will create endurance. It won't always guarantee you'll be a winner, but it will almost always guarantee you'll be a survivor.

10

#2: Build Structure in the Struggle

Structure gives you direction and focus. Every day of my life, I wanted better—to do better, to be better. I wanted to make sure I didn't just sit back while life passed me by. To do that, I realized I had to get up and do something about it. Any moment that came across my path that allowed me to better myself was an opportunity I'd take. I wasn't going to be ashamed of where I was, because it was who I'd become that mattered.

I had the desire to change my life. I knew what I wanted, and I was willing to put in the work to get it. This might seem shocking to some, but that alone is not enough. You can grind your wheels and find yourself spinning out in the same place you've always been. If I wanted to truly change my life, I had to make sure that my efforts were focused on the right application. For that I would need structure.

There are some aspects of the foster care system that I disliked. Splitting my family up would be one of them. However, overall, my time in the system wasn't a negative experience. More than anything it gave me the gift and knowledge of the power of structure.

Being in the environment I was as a child, having certain securities provided to you like food or a bed can make all the difference. For me, it gave me the space to think about more than just my survival. I didn't have to become a product of my environment. I had options and choices. That mindset would equip me well just a few years later.

By the time I reached the age of about ten or eleven, I was no longer in foster care. I had found my way back home, where figuring out ways to keep a refrigerator full was still near the top of my mind. It was a common problem that I was familiar with. This time, things would be different. What changed was my approach to how I thought of solving that problem. In order to get food, you had to have the means to purchase it. That meant money.

I learned of ways you could earn money while in foster care. There was a program where you could go down to the *Commercial Appeal*, a Memphis newspaper, to grab papers to sell on the street corner. They had a deal where you could grab a bundle of about twenty newspapers and sell them for two dollars apiece. The take-home for each paper was about twenty-five cents. That might not seem like much, but when you are willing to hustle and put in the work, that can add up. Having that option was a blessing. It meant that I could choose to do the right thing in order to fill my belly. I wouldn't have to go down the spiraling path of bad choices just to eat.

After foster care, I didn't return to school. There was a year when it would just be me and the streets. Without school you lose out on five free lunches a week. I knew I would have to make some money if I wanted to eat. In remembering the work I did with the *Commercial Appeal*, I decided to call up the people who I had sold with during my time in foster care. Somehow, I had saved their number. They agreed to help me out. I think they were pleased to see me trying to earn my way honestly just like them.

I relied on them to drive me to the paper to pick up my bundles. I would typically pick up about ten bundles at a time before heading out east. When you're selling papers for two dollars a pop, you aren't selling them in the hood. I would go to the wealthy white neighborhoods like Germantown. My two corners were on Winchester Road between Riverdale and Kirby. The sells weren't easy. You had to work for them. More than anything you had to seem approachable—put on a smile and be positive. That taught me the people skills I would need to get by in life. I could sell out of my ten to twenty bundles in a day. When you do the math, it's about fifty to a hundred dollars for the week to spend on food and other necessities.

Learning how to earn my own money was only one aspect of structure that I picked up from foster care. Another discipline of structure that I would carry with me would be scheduling. For a ten-year-old that was as simple as setting a bedtime of 9:00 p.m. and waking up before 7:00 a.m. It might not seem like a lot, but that discipline would set me up for success once I got the opportunity to go to Briarcrest just four years later.

...

Education that benefits requires structure. It is one of the most distinguishable differences between private and public school systems. I'm not talking about just plain old organization. I'm talking about real-life, saturating structure.

In public school, I had my classes and homework. There were periods assigned to different subjects. I would wake up every morning, get on the bus, and go to school. At the end of the day, I would get off at the same time. That was the limit of structure I found at public school. As soon as I stepped off the bus, any help or structure that had existed at school would be gone. And that was the problem. There were some nights when I wouldn't even have a home to come back to.

Outside of school, there was no one helping me develop

structure. Even at school, the teachers were stretched so thin that they didn't have a clue about what went on after I left their class. It wasn't their fault. When you teach thousands of kids on limited resources, sometimes the best you can give can just fall short.

I recognized the gap of structure missing in my life. Even before Tony or Briarcrest came along, I tried to create what I could with what I had. I knew that my education was important. So I wanted to make sure I woke up on time to get to school every single day. I used the few dollars I had to buy that alarm clock. It was the only way I knew how to provide the routine I needed to accomplish my goals.

That discipline followed me to Briarcrest. Once I got the opportunity to attend private school, everything started to change. There were many factors that elevated my performance at Briarcrest. Most of those that differed from my time at public school were the intangibles: fellow classmates' attitude, the teachers' attention to individual performance, and uniformed dress. Each one of those aspects added more structure to my life. What would follow would be the discipline I needed to raise my scores.

• • •

Structure plus effort equals progress. This was especially true when studying for one of the most difficult subjects I faced in school—math. History, English, and science weren't issues for me. All it took was time and dedication and I could learn the material. Math, on the other hand, was a different beast altogether. When I moved from public school to private, I faced a significant curriculum jump. Math went from having only numbers to including symbols, letters, and the Greek alphabet. I was in new territory.

The year this change took place, I had Ms. Nowicki as my math teacher. She would be there on my journey to master her class. I can remember dedicating hours a night to homework in that class. Just one problem could take the better part of two hours to complete. Passing that class took dedication, but I did it.

Facing that challenge in Ms. Nowicki's class taught me a valuable lesson. It had nothing to do with solving quadratic equations. Learning the subject gave me a blueprint for how I should approach certain problems in my life. There is no talking your way through a math problem at that level. You have to start from the beginning and get to work. You have to put pencil to paper and begin the long process of working it out in front of you—one systematic step at a time. By the end you will have solved your problem. Let me tell you, there was no greater joy or sense of accomplishment than the feeling I got whenever I solved one of the problems in her class.

There are many hurdles and walls in life that are like that math problem. You may be facing that insurmountable or impossible feat in front of you. You don't have a way out. Your only option is to move forward. Start taking action one step at a time, in an organized way. Don't give up, and with determination and perseverance you will find yourself with the solution you were looking for.

I am always thankful for those kinds of lessons in life. The intellectual challenges I took on as a kid helped build the mental stamina that I use to solve problems every single day. Ones that require critical thinking and intellect. Problems like educating youth who find themselves at a socioeconomic disadvantage.

...

Structure prepares you for the walls you have yet to face. Whether it was learning how to provide for myself with integrity, having the discipline to wake up on time for school, or passing my algebra class, I was laying the building blocks of practiced structure.

Now, after having moved beyond the walls in my own life, I can use my skill set to help others move beyond the walls they face.

That is what I am building at the Oher Foundation—programs that provide structure for kids who haven't been given that resource. My approach to finding a solution for these kids is in a lot of ways no different than the homework I had back in high school. However, I doubt your need for reading these lessons on finding your way forward is for schoolwork.

When you find yourself backed up against a wall, building an organized approach through practiced discipline and purposeful action toward a solution gives you the road map you need to move forward. As with anything in life, there are many factors that play into your experiences. That is why, unlike homework, real-life scenarios require you to seek help and get others in the boat with you. That was a valuable lesson I learned throughout my life, which was later solidified by my friend Matt Birk.

Starting a foundation based on education for the youth is a big undertaking. It requires a sizable number of resources and team effort in order to get off the ground. That is why I turned to Matt for guidance. Not only did I respect him for his intellect, being voted "the sixth smartest athlete" of all time by the *Sporting News* in 2010, but he also had personal experience in starting up his own school. His advice to me was this:

Ask for help. Seek counsel.

The man who graduated from Harvard, played in the NFL, and started his own school was telling me to ask for help and seek counsel. If the most qualified person was telling me this, then it should tell you something very important. I would take his advice and talk to consulting educators, school founders, leaders in the social work field. It takes humility to ask a question, and it takes humility to listen to the answer. It also takes discipline to catalog what you've learned. But most important, it isn't about what you know, it's about understanding when to seek help and knowing who to go to.

There is never a time in your life when you will face a challenge or wall that you were meant to surmount on your own. We were designed for community and relationship. Tackling problems is supposed to be a team effort. So surrounding yourself with the right people to depend on for your life's challenges becomes as important as injecting structure into your struggle. This is why my next lesson discusses the importance of the people you keep by your side.

11

#3: Have a Small Circle

There's an African proverb that says, "If you want to go fast, you go alone. If you want to go far, you go together."

Believe it or not, my instincts are to go alone. It's natural to want to put yourself in an environment where you are fully in control. Team sports aren't like that. You have to rely and count on others on a team. That takes faith. Football, like a lot of team sports, is tricky. To succeed, you have to move like a unit. A football team has eleven people on the field at any given time. Eleven people working in unison. Eleven people who've pushed aside the problems of their day and are ready to play.

It takes trust to be part of a team. Each time I leveled up, I didn't just have to think about my own performance. I also had to think about the next guy—his thoughts, his preparation, his physical strengths. This means more factors beyond my control—more that I had to let go of.

I figured that out quickly when I left high school and went to Ole Miss. The greater the talent, the greater the pressure, the greater the chance for distraction. I was there on a scholarship, and I took that seriously. I was no-nonsense. Ready to work. I was getting a free education. Food to eat, books to study, a bed to sleep on—this was a good gig for me, and I wasn't about to mess up and have that taken away.

My ability to maintain that privilege rested on my teammates as well. I had to depend on their readiness to play. I found that a little nerve-racking—having to depend on someone else for my dream.

We go farther when we are not alone. It might be simpler to fly solo sometimes. Living on an island might be more predictable and even convenient, but you miss out on a lot of things, like the beauty of experiencing something as a team.

I knew what I had signed up for. I was a football player, so I quickly started thinking of ways to gel with my team. One thing that helped me was my positive mindset. This time, I didn't apply it to just myself, I applied it to those around me. I chose to believe the best about everybody—their motivations and their skill sets. I thought better about my teammates than some of them even thought about themselves. It wasn't about ego; it was about believing in their capabilities and using them to show up for each other.

This little trick was particularly helpful with interactions between offense and defense. For a competitive person, the sidelines can be tough. You don't want to just stand there, you want to *do* something. Even if we weren't having the greatest season, I always believed the best about our team. "Our defense is the best defense in the world," I'd say to everybody. I expect my guys not to give up a yard or a point. I have faith they can do it. Once you're my guy, I'm locked in with you, and when something goes wrong, I'm legitimately surprised. That attitude has helped me go against my natural instinct and "buy in," even when our record isn't something to write home about.

But here's where I need to make an important distinction. Your circle isn't your team. It's much smaller than that. A circle is the tight group of people who get you. Whose influence supports and sustains you. I had a group of like-minded guys back at Briarcrest, but I didn't find my true circle until later on. You can't always choose your teams—your coworkers, your neighbors even—but you choose who is in your circle. For a long time, I thought one's circle had to be immediate family. I didn't realize it was a choice. One of the most important choices I could ever make. I meet good people every day. But at this point, I don't pull people out of my circle and put other people in.

Relational energy is a resource. True friendship lets people in, lets them sharpen you. And that can be dangerous, and sometimes it can hurt. Like the proverb says, "The wounds of a friend are faithful." I believe that, but it means I'm going to be pretty choosy about who I let "wound" me, so to speak.

Don't hear this as me advocating for cliques. I think everyone should be treated with the same level of decency and respect regardless of their status or trade. Until someone gives you reason not to, you should treat them as your equal.

There is a need in this world for basic human respect. For us to see people for who they really are. Your circle can be anywhere. Your people—the people you really gel with—might be in an unlikely place. You've got to have your head up for them.

And you don't need that many close friends. When times really get rough, if you think the people you can count on are on two hands, you're mistaken. Your true circle is actually small. Look for quality over quantity. Like Pastor Dale loves to remind me: "A man of many companions may come to ruin, but there is a friend who sticks closer than a brother."

• • •

That is why I think Robert De Niro had it right when, in his great movie *Meet the Parents*, he was harassing his new son-in-law: *The small circle is a circle of trust.*

Again, when I think about that fact, I've got to bring it back to Matt Birk.

I said I always felt most at home playing on the road. One reason for that was Birk and I had a deal. He'd never admit this (because, he insists, we are peers), but I was his student. I respected his views on the game. Matt trusted my instincts, and one way he proved that to me was to occasionally let me pick the snap count when we were on the road.

For the uninitiated, let me explain why that was significant.

When you are playing at home, at your own stadium, the fans obviously want you to do well. They are quieter, so you can hear the snap count. But on the road, all that courtesy goes out the window. The fans from the opposing team are doing everything they can to break your concentration (and your eardrums). It's so loud that all the cheering becomes one giant roar in your ears. It's impossible to hear, so on the road, your snap count is often silent. Seeing as how I was good at reading defenders and I had a good vantage point, Birk would sometimes defer to me.

"What do you want it on?" he'd ask.

I'd give him my answer, and nine times out of ten, we were able to get guys to jump offsides. It might be a simple thing, but the trust he had in me took me far.

• • •

Like I said way back when I was talking about being in Dr. Simpson's office, one of the good things the streets did for me was teach me how to read people. I studied them. I could get a sense of who wanted me around. I could also sense when people were truly welcoming and when they wanted me to get lost, and that struggle helped me sense a genuine person from one who is not.

People aren't always who you think they are. I've found that if you have any amount of celebrity or notoriety attached to your name, your circle is even smaller than you think. The more people who wear your jersey and chant your name, the less you really feel seen sometimes. That inability to be known and understood can lead to athletes feeling depressed.

Having a true circle means a couple of things. Number one: You will be known. There's great risk and great reward in that. These people will see your flaws. That's the risk. But these people will also know the real you. For me, that's been invaluable. I'll admit that one of the hardest things about being in the public eye is that you can't correct the things people say about you that are untrue. Thanks to the power of the internet, anyone can spread whatever lie they want to, and some people will believe it's gospel truth. And it's out there permanently, for people to read and comment on. I don't care who you are, that kind of thing hurts.

But that's when you go back to your people. The people who truly know you and can affirm who you are.

You will be known (and even called out). But your character will not grow in the presence of "yes people." When you lose your way, your circle can call you back.

And there's no better example of that than the friend I met as an incoming freshman at Ole Miss, Jamarca Sanford.

When he tells people about me, Jamarca likes to say I was "the brother he never had, but was always looking for." I was the opposite. I had a lot of brothers. I honestly wasn't looking for more until I met him. There is a lot of pressure when you're coming into a university to play sports. You think you know the game, but overnight you're tossed into a much bigger pond, and there is so much to prove. For a person like me, who constantly has the shadow of other people hanging over him, it was an intense time. Not everybody understood the pressures I was feeling. But that was the cool thing about Jamarca. He always took the game of football as seriously as I did. When I got to Oxford, he'd already been red-shirted for a year, so in 2005, we both came in hungry and ready to play.

But also like me, Jamarca liked to joke around. Our lives would parallel in ways I couldn't have guessed back then.

We both went on to play in the NFL. We were on different teams, but we were in the league for almost the same time. Jamarca, like me, would suffer an injury and go on injured reserve. His was different—hip and a sports hernia—but still, five surgeries in three years is no small thing. He used to joke with me, "At least you still got your hips!"

We kept each other afloat as we transitioned from professional football. As much as anybody could get down in the trenches with me during my darkest hour, Jamarca did.

There are friends you have for certain seasons. Some really close friends are part of your life only for a certain amount time, and that's okay. We all go through times when our friend group gets pruned. You go through a serious tragedy, your circle will shrink down even more.

Part of why my circle is small has to do with what Jamarca says about me: "Big Dawg is gonna stick to his routine and what he wants to do. You're not gonna make him do anything he doesn't want to."

He is right. I'm not the type to listen to the crowd. I've never truly felt pressured to go against my own way of thinking just to be cool.

• • •

Jamarca's wasn't the only lifelong friendship that came from my time in Oxford. One of the most important relationships in my life started at Ole Miss. Because I'm loyal and protective of my circle, I don't share my personal life with the public. My in-house family is the most important part of my world. I know how vicious it can be. I know how unkind it can be, and because of that, I've protected them fiercely from the cruel and careless words of strangers.

If I'm talking about my circle, my wife, Tiffany, is in the center of it. Her presence in my life is truly like my foundation: strong and stabilizing, but not always seen.

Our story is a funny one. One that I haven't shared a lot about. It wasn't love at first sight, at least not on her end. And like everything else good in my life, it wasn't handed to me. I had to work for it.

...

It all started at the registrar's office at Ole Miss. It was 2007, and I was in my junior year. Like I've said, ever since Briarcrest, I had been obsessed with my academic record. I'm a competitor. I'm the kind of guy who needs to see tangible success. So I went down to the registrar to request a transcript, and there was a cute girl working the window.

The first thing I noticed about her was that she didn't seem to care I was an athlete. Some girls look at you and talk to you in a different way if they realize you play football. I assumed she dealt with athletes and their grades all the time when I thanked her for her help and she just nodded and turned away without batting an eye.

Days later, the cute girl at the window kept coming to mind, so even though I didn't really need another transcript, I got the twenty-five cents it cost for a paper copy and went down to the registrar to see her again.

She wasn't there, so I asked another, older lady about her, describing a gorgeous short girl.

"You mean Tiffany?" the woman said.

"Yes, ma'am." I nodded. "Tiffany."

"She isn't here today."

I thanked the woman and counted it as my first victory. At least I had her name.

A few days passed, and I went to the registrar again. This time, she was there.

"I heard you came here asking about me," Tiffany said coolly. "I mean, I figured it was you, but nobody knew your name."

Since it was clear she wasn't interested in giving me *her* contact info, I slid my cell number through the window and hoped she would call.

She didn't.

I waited some more. Like I've been preaching since the beginning, nine times out of ten, the name of any game worth playing is patience.

It took a few weeks and, finally, she called. I almost didn't answer it, because when I looked at the caller ID, the number was blocked.

There was a realness to her that I liked. As a football player, I received plenty of attention from other girls. But that kind of attention isn't real. They are so taken with your college level of celebrity fame as an athlete that they often forget to care about the person behind the talent. Tiffany, on the other hand, was authentic. She had this self-respect about her. She wasn't going to just jump at the first sign of a guy being interested in her. I admired that kind of self-respect and reserve.

We took things slow, but after a few months we were talking regularly. It was a short walk from Vaught-Hemingway Stadium to the Martindale Student Services Center, where the registrar was located, and I was burning up the path. I finally had a person I could consistently share my heart with. I could talk to her about whatever pressures I was dealing with. Unlike most of my other friends, Tiffany didn't have any context for me. She was a little bit older than me, and she was from New Orleans, so my hometown was worlds away as far as she was concerned. Nothing about me had reached her. No Hurt Village, no Briarcrest, not even the excitement surrounding my recruitment to Ole Miss. Her disinterest in all of that was refreshing. We could just talk about normal stuff. She also gave good advice.

Eventually over time, she would slowly get to know my story. But the things that would impress a normal person were like water off a duck's back with Tiffany. She was interested in *me*, not any of the flashy sound bites that surrounded me. Her personality wasn't going to change just because of some "fame." I fell in love with that.

Today we've been together almost sixteen years. During that time, many people have asked Tiffany if she had any reservations about dating a "famous" football player, especially since she is such a private person. I guess if you judge based on those personality tests, I'm more of an introvert, but Tiffany is that way even more so. While we were living in Baltimore, she was approached by a TV show. The theme of the show had something to do with the lives of NFL wives. A lot of girls would do anything for that kind of attention, but Tiffany just rolled her eyes. She valued the private time she got with her family instead.

No surprise, Tiffany doesn't have Facebook, and to this day, she barely uses Instagram. Her presence on social media is so small, I've even been told that there was some kind of website dedicated to trying to decide if Michael Oher's "wife" was actually a real person. That's how much she avoids the spotlight. But what I love and respect about her is that she doesn't need me to be a part of her identity. I can't tell you how invaluable it has been to have that kind of person in my circle. Someone who is genuine. Who is not self-serving. Who signed up for the journey before the movie had hit the theaters. When I was just Michael, not the football player from *The Blind Side*.

In the ways that matter, she is the same down-to-earth woman she was in the registrar's office when she didn't really want to give me the time of day. We left Oxford together and went on from there. Baltimore, Nashville, Charlotte, and back to Nashville.

Her support is part of what has kept me grounded for whatever road is ahead.

···

A circle is just one resource in your tool belt of life. Even though it is one of your most powerful resources, it's never your only option.

Sometimes the thing that separates those who make it in those back-against-the-wall moments simply comes down to their ability to understand what they have and how they can use it.

I know there are going to be some out there, particularly young kids, who might feel like they haven't found their circle yet. I've been there, and I'll tell you, that can be one of the hardest things to wait for, but it's worth the wait. Pay attention. Keep your head up for genuine people. The ones who get you.

And while you are waiting, take stock of your own life. Be the kind of person someone else wants in their circle. If networking is the key that opens doors, you want to be someone meaningful who people want to get to know.

12

#4: Use What You've Got

When I ask young kids what they hope for themselves, a lot of times I hear the same thing: "Well, I don't know. . . . I'm just . . . ordinary."

It's funny to me that our society thinks there are huge genetic differences between us. Maybe it's a product of TV—we love the story of the unassuming kid who turns out to have some sort of supernatural skill—but that's just not reality. The way I see it, genetics have been elevated at the expense of effort. What do I mean? I mean you can work with "ordinary."

There are two ways in which I see ordinary at play. The first of them has to do with background and upbringing. Your circumstances can be average—or worse, they can be downright bad. You can still use them. Let me explain.

I have a concept that has helped me, but it can trip people up at first. I call it the "anti–role model" model. Some people will tell you to go find a mentor. And that's great. For many people, that's just what they need. As I told the kids at Big Oak, when I was young, sometimes just knowing what was "right" was the bulk of my challenge. I was flying blind from a character standpoint, but I had the radio on. My antenna was up. I was constantly listening and evaluating, trying to find someone who I could pattern after. But there, at Big Oak, with loving houseparents, they had the cheat code.

What I am saying is more than just finding a mentor. I'm saying use what you've got.

A lot of kids in underprivileged situations don't have the luxury of a good mentor already in their lives. That doesn't mean they shouldn't try to find one. For years, I looked and looked, but all I could see were bad examples.

But that didn't stop me from learning from people. That shouldn't stop you from learning from people, either. Sometimes people mistakenly think mentors are going to give them all the answers. That's not always the case. If you have them, use them. If not, be independent. Learn from other people's mistakes. You don't have to get too close to see where they're going wrong.

As a kid, here is what I saw from the men in my community:
They were high.
They were disrespectful of women.
They didn't provide for our basic needs.
They were late (if they showed up at all).
Their highest goals were minimum-wage jobs.
This isn't a difficult concept. It's simple, really. As I got older, I made it my mission to look at that list and do the opposite. There are a lot of disadvantages of the digital age, but here's one way the connectivity has served us well: You don't have to know your mentors personally. The average kid can go on the internet and he's face-to-face with his hero. I remember the days of sitting on the floor watching Michael Jordan. I learned from him. How he carried himself on the court. How he talked in interviews. I've never met MJ, but I always joke that I don't want to. I'm the kind of guy who doesn't want to meet his heroes. I was always afraid that if I talked to somebody, I would ruin it. But Jordan? Okay, maybe one day I could shake his hand while he was walking past

in a crowd. I'd shake it and keep going. That would be good enough.

The point is that Jordan was my mentor when I didn't have one. I used what I had, even if it was someone off in the periphery.

There's a video that went viral on Twitter of a white coach at a kids' summer camp who did an illustration trying to show his mostly white, blessed campers what life is like for others who don't start out with the same advantages.

He lined all the kids up in a field and said, "Okay, we are going to have a race, and the winner of the race will take this. . . ."

He pulled a hundred-dollar bill from his pocket. "But before we get started, I'm going to make a few statements. If those statements apply to you, take two steps forward. If they don't apply to you, stay right where you are."

The kids lined up, and like the game Mother May I? the statements began.

Take two steps forward if your parents are still married.

Take two steps forward if you have a father figure in your home.

Take two steps forward if you've never had to help with the bills.

Take two steps forward if you've never had to worry about your next meal.

As you might expect, a lot of the kids were almost to the finish line before the race began. While other kids—many of them Black males—were still standing where they started.

At the end of the statements, the coach looked at the kids staggered across the field and turned his attention to the ones in front. "I want you to turn around. Nothing you have done has put you in the lead right now."

The kids in the front looked around.

"There is no excuse." He pointed to the brothers in the back. "They've still got to run their race. . . . But some of us would be foolish not to realize that we've been given more opportunity."

The bottom line is this: We might have all been created equal, but the situations we were born into are not. Like those kids on the field, we need to recognize that fact. If you were lucky enough to start off ahead, if you have extraordinary natural ability, if you have resources and mentorship—use those advantages. Seize them, don't squander them. Let them lead you to excel, and then look back. Turn around and help the next guy.

But if you are like me, if life had you starting several steps behind everybody else, if your support system is ordinary, or just plain bad, you still have to run your race. So run as hard and as fast as you can. Take stock of everything around you and use it—all of it.

• • •

The other way you can work with ordinary is your own physical condition.

I saw this at work my first season at Briarcrest, playing under Coach Hugh Freeze. I've said this, but the small, white athletes at our private school were not the most talented kids in Memphis— not by a long shot. It was the coaching that lifted ordinary players up to another level. Got us out of our own way.

This concept was a real aha moment for me. I'd come up watching videos of Hall of Fame players. I thought I could muscle my way to the next level. But Coach Freeze was my first real example of playing smarter, not harder. The guy was (and still is) an offensive genius. At Briarcrest (and at Ole Miss), he knew how to utilize a team's strengths. He was new to the school my first year of high school, but he recognized right away that he had some smart players at Briarcrest, so he used that to his advantage. He elevated our playbook. It was not uncommon for us to have as many as three plays ready in a huddle. That is pretty unusual for a high school team, but we pulled it off with guidance from Coach Freeze. That level of mental depth and understanding of the game was something I hadn't experienced at the other schools I'd attended. We could never have had multiple plays ready. Somebody would have been like, "Time-out, time-out!" so they could remember what was coming next.

Point being, it's not always about the raw materials; it's what you do with them. Average with the right guidance will evolve into excellence. And in football, if you've got good coaching, you can get better. If you've got the right philosophies, techniques, and fundamentals like Coach Freeze does, it's possible to take what you have all the way to a championship.

What was true for the Briarcrest team was actually true for me personally. I always say this: I was never the most talented guy on the football field. Even in the small pond back in Memphis, I knew I wasn't extraordinary. Now that I'm older and I know myself (and my body), I'm the first to admit that I'm no superstar. I knew this all the way back in the weight room with Marshay Green when he jokingly asked, "What's so special about Mike?"

Marshay's question is something that has empowered me in my adult life. It's something I take on the road when I talk to audiences. I joke about how, growing up, I could look at everyone in my birth family and never find anyone who could walk and chew bubble gum at the same time. We didn't have natural athletic talent. I wasn't born with a head start, physically speaking. It's frustrating because I know plenty of people who are just the opposite. My buddy Jamarca is one of them. We'll have a good time over the weekend, maybe eat some barbecue, and he gets back on Monday to his same old self—lean and mean. But I step on the scale and I've gained ten pounds!

What am I getting at? Most of us are born average, but what sets us apart is what we do with what we've got. Just because other guys like Jamarca have the metabolism of a cheetah doesn't mean I can make excuses for having to put in more time in the gym. It just means that I have to put more effort in and pay closer attention to what works and doesn't work for my body. If you are a young kid right now and thinking you are nothing special, I will tell you that the ordinary guy—with effort and consistency— can shine.

...

Sometimes working with ordinary means not overcomplicating things. It means you can keep it simple, but be consistent and flawless in your technique.

I can think of several all-star quarterbacks who exemplify this. If you're good, you don't need to be tricky. Take Peyton Manning. He's arguably one of the greatest quarterbacks of all time. Guess what he does? He steps back into the pocket, and then he steps up again. I get fired up when I think about the consistency of his technique. Too bad we were never on the same team because blocking for Peyton Manning would have been the perfect match for me. Like Tom Brady and the Patriots, it would have been a nice pairing. Brady actually started imitating Manning with his pocket awareness. Both of those guys had limited fitness skills, so they figured out how to use protection. I'm not implying that either of these men were anything but extraordinary. I'm simply trying to suggest that while they might not have been born as versatile as Cam Newton, they more than made up for it. Sometimes the GOATs (Greatest Of All Time) are just clean and consistent. They're not set apart from birth. They didn't fall from the planet Krypton. They have allowed ordinary to mature into excellence over time.

....

I have a reputation with my in-house family for being hard on the kids, particularly when it comes to academics. My wife, Tiffany, says to friends, "Michael's tough when it comes to schoolwork. He's always had expectations for our kids. He's hard on them because he's hard on himself."

She is right. I hold all of my kids, Kobi, Kierstin, MJ, and Naivi, to the same standards. There were—and still are—no Cs or Ds allowed in our house. Maybe that sounds harsh, but I believe it's fair because they are capable. It's the amount of effort you put in that will determine the outcome. If one method isn't working for you and you're not getting the results you want, have the tenacity to find another way. I preach this like the gospel truth because I lived it out. And when it comes to truly difficult situations, it is even more true.

What I've overcome, others can, too. Everyone has a spark. If given the right situation, they can light it up. I believe we are all born with a fighter's mentality; you just have to know how to find it.

There's a saying that goes something like this: A poor carpenter blames his tools. I'd have to agree with that. Do not use your situation as a crutch. Make the most of it. Every average Joe can change the world. It just takes time—and patience.

Make the goal. Make a plan, and then another plan—then execute it. Throw out the timeline and wait.

Be consistent. Be resourceful. Be patient. Ordinary can be extraordinary in five years' time.

13

#5: Be Relentlessly Positive

A rising tide lifts all boats.
—John F. Kennedy

When John F. Kennedy said these words to the American people, he was talking about the economy. But I'd say it applies to attitude just as well.

Attitude is contagious, so you want to be around people who lift you. And likewise, be somebody who lifts others.

I swear you can spot a positive person from a mile away. You can be in the Starbucks line and see it. Attitude is contagious. Wherever you go, you are spreading your attitude, and that attitude can make people feel sick or feel well.

When I was a little kid, even though I might not have been able to articulate it, I realized this principle. I realized that positivity was a rudder. I woke up each day knowing that almost everything I was going to face was going to be out of my hands: what I ate (if I ate), where I slept, who I was around. The list went on and on. These external factors could have left me feeling powerless, but I knew there was something inside me I could control. The most powerful tool in the belt: my mindset. Just like I suggested with want-to, when your back's against the wall, you will see more answers if you are looking through a positive lens.

....

If you aren't positive, chances are you have small dreams.

Think about that for a minute. Negativity limits you. It's wall after wall of "I can't, it won't, I'll never . . ."

As an eighth grader on a rubbly blacktop in the projects, I told everyone I was gonna "go pro" right out of high school. I wasn't talking football; I was talking basketball. I told everyone I was going to make it, and I believed it. I played better because of it. People around me might have thought I was a little crazy, but nobody could take my mindset from me.

I sometimes tell a joke when I give speeches. I say, "The NFL held me back. I was motivated to do something great."

What I mean by that is, I was always going to dream the biggest possible dreams. As you get older, it gets harder and harder to dream. That's not news to anyone. Each roadblock chips away at the dream. Each hard "No" we get in life makes us more of a cynic, so you've got to fight to stay hopeful. It's like I said with want-to: Your body language regulates your energy. People think I'm joking, but I have this saying now. If you got out on the wrong side of the bed, get back in and roll out on the other side. You gotta position yourself with enthusiasm. Keep dreaming big dreams.

In the same way, being relentlessly positive can also mean choosing to ignore the facts. Since I'm at a place in my life where I'm trying to move into the field of education, I feel like I have also shifted back into a student's mindset. I'm constantly reading and looking at the research. But here's something about being positive: Sometimes you need to trash the research. You need to ignore the reasonable, probable, even the practical, and you need to let your belief be what carries you into the next day. Positivity is sometimes blind to the odds.

There's a lot out there about my past. When I look at my childhood, not much of it is happy. But if I try, I can sometimes find some positive mile markers as well. I think it's important to remember those. For me, the list was short but meaningful.

Probably the first thing that comes to mind is how much time I got to spend outside. Living in the hood, we got to play a lot. We were outdoors all the time. In Hurt Village, inside the house was not exactly comfortable, especially in the heat of summertime when the window units weren't working right. I think about it a lot now. I love my neighborhood in Nashville, but most of the time you don't see other people in their yards. That's the thing about rich people. They have everything they need inside, all self-contained, so there's not as much reason to go out. But there's a lot of living waiting for you outside your front door, and living in the hood forced us to figure that out.

Growing up the way I did also provided me a lot of freedom, especially at the first of the month when the government checks came out. My mother would be gone, so my siblings and I would float between friends. It was a survival skill I learned almost as early as I could walk, or at least as early as I could reason. This sounds like a bad thing—and most of the time it was—but it also made me independent and able to communicate with people. From very early on, I *had* to talk.

I had to ask for food. I had to ask for shelter. I had to communicate the needs of my siblings to my community. Basically, I had to think on my feet. It might be hard to view that as a positive thing, but now I can appreciate that the situation forced me to take control. It's true what they say: A homeless boy is a grown man by the age of ten. As difficult as it was, sometimes I liked the challenge of overseeing my own destiny.

• • •

Sometimes positivity looks like encouragement. This is a simple example, but ever since I was a kid, if a person slips and falls, I don't laugh first. I check on them. You don't know what people are dealing with internally. When I was in the NFL, I was surrounded by dudes who thought they had to be Superman. They had to have that cape on. Show no weakness. When one of our teammates showed a moment of weakness—a chink in the armor, so to speak—they were immediately met with ridicule. It is hard to be in a place where everyone is expected to be on their game all the time. The encouragement can turn someone on like a light switch.

I like to laugh and cut up as much as the next guy, but sometimes hold your jokes and just be kind first. Laugh later. Criticize later. You'd be surprised at the kind of loyalty this will win you. Take it from me. I've been on both sides of that equation.

Positive people are encouraging people. This can be applied in a thousand different ways. Not long ago, I was riding my bike through some trails outside of Franklin, Tennessee. I was stopped at a crossroads in the path and this little Black kid came barreling down the hill on his bike. He was coming straight for me, but then he swerved and just missed me. A few seconds later, a white dude came after him on his bike, yelling, "Son, slow down!"

I kept riding, but something told me to turn around and talk to them. I felt a special pull, maybe because it was a white dad and a Black son. When I caught up with them, the dad immediately started apologizing for the kid almost running me over. I told them it was no big deal, and then I turned to the son. "You know, I was taken in by a white family too."

The dad's face lit up. "I knew you looked familiar! You're Michael Oher!" He turned to his son. "Remember that movie we watched about that adopted football player? This is him!" He pulled out his phone and started reading off my stats. "He's from Memphis. . . . He won a Super Bowl. . . ."

The boy, who was about seven or eight, smiled at me. It was a cool moment. It always feels good to encourage people who come up to me and want to talk about adoption. You might think that is crazy, considering some of the grievances I've aired, but despite any complexities that have come from my own personal story, I wholeheartedly believe in adoption. Adoption is a good thing. It's part of what I hope to dedicate the rest of my life to, and I will always be an advocate for those looking to adopt. Anytime someone comes up to me—especially a foster parent—and tells me that they had the courage to adopt because of *The Blind Side*, I feel so overwhelmed with gratitude. One thing my story did that was undeniably positive was that it gave people the freedom to act on something tugging at their hearts. So I encourage them. I tell them what a good thing they did. The white parents I know personally who have adopted Black kids did so out of love. They did not stand by and let the complexity of the situation be a cop-out for them to do nothing.

Whatever the color of your skin, need is need. Hunger is color-blind. Hopelessness is color-blind. Interracial adoption is complicated. I'm not suggesting it's easy. People can debate about the complications of it all day long: *White people shouldn't adopt Black kids because they'll never understand Black culture,* and that kind of thing. Everyone is entitled to their opinion, but the message I want to share—particularly for parents involved in interracial adoption—is just a word of encouragement. It's simple and it's positive: You did the right thing.

You can deal with the complicated stuff later, like figuring out where to get their hair cut. There is a learning curve and constant issues to deal with, but if you simplify the equation, what you're left with is an act of love.

That's just one example of many of the social situations that people argue about these days. Sometimes you have to stop and ask, how much time do we waste crafting the perfect argument for a Facebook comment? And what good is being done while we are sitting at a computer screen? Who is going hungry while we are making the perfect comeback?

What would the world look like if we were positive first? If we found a way to encourage before we critiqued?

• • •

Sometimes positivity means you've got to actively cut out the negatives.

Like an old coach of mine once said: Remove your mental weights.

The National Science Foundation estimates that the average person can think up to sixty thousand thoughts in a day. The research also says of those thoughts, 80 percent are negative and 95 percent are repetitive.

So where does that leave us? With 45,600 negative thoughts bombarding you every day—that's some weight! It's not surprising that you can't get out of a tough situation if you are on the hamster wheel of hating on yourself.

Think negative things all the time, and negative things follow you. What you think, you manifest. When you're in a back-against-the-wall situation, if you believe it is impossible, I promise you, you're right. It is.

There's a saying by an old Chinese philosopher, Lao Tzu: "Watch your thoughts; they become words. Watch your words; they become actions. Watch your actions; they become habit. Watch your habits; they become character. Watch your character; it becomes your destiny."

Let's boil that down: Thoughts equal destiny. I believe that with my whole heart. It's like I said to those kids at Big Oak, "Whatever you want your future to be, you've got to change your thoughts right now."

I had to remind myself of that recently. Not long ago, I could not walk twenty-five yards without having to stop and catch my breath. Twenty-five yards is the length of a swimming pool. That was humbling, especially considering a few years before that I had been able to run the 40 in 5.34 seconds. But I had to believe I would get back there. I didn't give any mental real estate to doubt.

...

Sometimes being positive means putting an end date to your grieving.

Leaving the NFL was a difficult stage in my life. I didn't go out by choice. I loved football. I still had fire in me physically. I wasn't ready to leave the game. I loved my position on the offensive line. I loved my team. I loved Charlotte. I had just signed a three-year extension on my contract.

No matter how blessed you are, it's still hard to have something you love taken from you without your say, before you're ready. Football was my stabilizing force. It was a constant when things were tough. It was like an anchor.

So my disappointing (and sudden) exit from the game was a place in my own life where I had to choose to be positive. That doesn't mean you don't grieve a loss. You do. But then, at some point, you've got to take the exit off the freeway of feeling sorry for yourself. Choose to look for the bright side of your bad situation. And don't do that in the abstract. Put that stuff down on paper. Count your blessings by name. Put them in a place where you see them every day.

For me, that list is long. Though my mind and body may never fully heal, I do have time. I get to be with my family. I get to talk about this game I love with my son. I get to use my energy for the betterment of kids I would have never been able to reach from the football field.

Were there dreams I still had for my time in the game? Absolutely.

Did I have to abandon my own Ray Lewis–size hopes for how I'd go out? No doubt. I had planned on being in the Hall of Fame. Laugh if you want to, but I was going to "go big" toward my dreams.

Other times, cutting out the negative looks like something else altogether. Something you might not expect: forgiveness. Hang with me here. This is an area of my life that is pretty big right now. I've already shared some past hurts that, if I'm being honest, are still pretty raw. I have wise people around me, mentors who have been handling conflict a lot longer than I have, and they've helped me view forgiveness in a different way.

Forgiveness doesn't mean you are a doormat. It also doesn't necessarily mean the relationship continues. I've spent a lot of time thinking about why forgiveness is so difficult for us, and the best way I can explain it is that it always comes at a cost. When there is an injury or a loss, somebody has to pay for it. If the person who is responsible for that injury doesn't "pay," there is a sort of injustice gap. In order for you to reconcile, both parties have to want it. The offending party has to take ownership of what they've done and, to use a biblical word, they have to repent. That is the equation. That's the only way for a damaged relationship to be mended.

For so long, I got frustrated with myself because I wanted to be the bigger person. I wanted to be able to forgive everyone for everything, right down to the people who'd hurt me as a kid. I wanted to do that because I truly desire other people's happiness. I want my life to be free of any kind of ill will. So I tried to do both roles, on both sides of the equation: to forgive the people who were not only unrepentant but were still actively hurting me. Just like in football, you cannot heal an injury that is still happening. No surprise, that left me pretty hurt. Like I was sitting on the emotional freeway and wondering why I kept getting hit.

As I've matured, I have realized that you can (and most of the time, you should) forgive someone who's not asking for it. But there will be no true reconciliation. That might seem like bad news, but it's actually very freeing. What it means is that you can forgive for your own sake. You can release the ultimate outcome of that damaged relationship. It doesn't erase the injury, but it means that you no longer have to be defined by it. You won't even realize how heavy your bitterness is until you drop it. It is like actual weight loss. Suddenly, without it, you can breathe. You can move. You are free to focus on and enjoy other things.

But if you cling to that hurt, if you keep feeding that anger, you are letting someone else control your narrative. I realized that the things I'm able to pursue right now—trying to impact kids, trying to motivate and change lives—none of that was going to happen unless I released some hurts from my past. When you are relentlessly positive, you are free to forgive those who don't deserve it. You are choosing the bright side.

But to be clear, that doesn't mean the relationship will be healed, but you will be.

There's an exercise I want you to try. Think of the thing in your life, the deepest unresolved hurt, the thing that's the hardest to forgive. Put your hands out and imagine it sitting there in your palms.

Now drop it. Whatever hurt you are holding on to, picture yourself physically releasing it.

If the person you are forgiving is unrepentant, you will never forget the hurt. I think people who tell you, "Forgive and forget," are fools. The wound will be crystal clear in your memory, but if you keep actively releasing the negativity—stop remembering and recounting the wrongs—you can find peace. You can forgive. Not because someone else deserves it, but because you deserve it.

The late Colin Powell, former secretary of state, is often quoted for his "13 Rules of Leadership." I found his number one rule to be similar to one of my own: *It ain't as bad as you think. It will look better in the morning.*

If that's true for a decorated officer—the first Black four-star general commanding troops—it's probably true for me and you.

When your back's against the wall, positivity is what will keep you afloat. You need it, and those around you need it. One word of encouragement can change someone's entire day, even their whole life. A rising tide lifts all ships.

14

#6: Heal Yourself First

Ahurt man is no help to anyone, even himself. This was a truth that was hard for me to accept for so long. There are many aspects of myself I identify with that would protest this proverb. Accepting vulnerability and your inability in a certain state isn't something that is easy to do, especially for a professional athlete who built his success on being the opposite. For so long, I had survived by becoming someone who aimed to please. As a kid I was an expert at masking my own needs for the sake of others. When you grow up knowing that most of your meals will come from other people's generosity, it's almost impossible not to be like this. For the sake of self-preservation, you learn early on to silence your own needs so that you can be whatever you have to be and do whatever is expected of you.

"Don't cause a problem." That's what I told myself time and again as a kid. The only truth I knew for sure was that if I did all that was asked of me and never let anybody down, things might turn out all right. So every ounce of energy I had I threw into working hard and not letting anybody down.

While there's merit in the decision to act selflessly, the consistent choice to prioritize others over my own needs became, at the very least, exhausting. When you are so worried about not disappointing the next guy, you can often push yourself past your own limits without even realizing it. Without the proper balance between selfless efforts and self-care, you can easily find yourself in a damaging position. That is what I saw with Kinnedy at the Big Oak Boys' Ranch. There was a kid who fiercely wanted to support his family, sometimes at the expense of his own future. Thankfully I would get to tell him the lesson I had only started to learn for myself.

"You have to heal yourself first. Everything else comes after."

...

Not every wall in life requires healing. Most of my early life was spent facing wall after wall. Every day was a fight to survive. I had to do battle against the odds just to make it that extra inch. It was a struggle, for sure. But when I was faced with those obstacles, I had two tools that could carry me past them—the strength of my mind and body.

Life doesn't always play out as planned. Beyond all adversity is an obstacle we will all have to face at one point or another in life. That wall is the obstacle of unhealth. It is uniquely different from all the other challenges you might face. The reason being, no matter how many challenges you have before you, if you are faced with the wall of ill health, discerning how to regain it will become your most vexing problem.

What do I mean by that? It's simple. Making your way around the other walls in life might require you to be in a healthy state. So if you all of a sudden find yourself or your health compromised, seeking a healthier you should become a priority if you hope to move forward again. This can be a difficult and complex task, mainly because your health isn't a state of being reserved only for your physical body. It can be used to describe your mental and emotional well-being, too. Finding your way to a healthier you in each case might look different. Just like different physical sicknesses require different medicines, your path beyond the walls of unhealth will require different treatments depending on which part of yourself has become unwell.

Physical injury or poor health can seem like the most extreme of the three. When you have a broken leg or are diagnosed with cancer, it is easy to understand what has caused your pain. At times the diagnosis can seem daunting. *How can I ever come back from this?* As scary as it might sound, the certainty of knowing your limitations can actually be a good thing. Your body is a tangible object. It can be touched, studied, and understood. It behaves according to laws of science. Even though that might not always mean there is a cure for what you are experiencing, more times than not there are answers for how you should proceed in life. My experience with this came, as you'd expect, in my NFL career.

· · ·

Something as small as a thorn can render a lion powerless. Many have heard of the fable of the thorn in the lion's toe that I shared earlier. What I had thought was a story told to children to teach a moral lesson actually had more truth behind it.

It took many years before I found myself in a position of vulnerability and helplessness, like the lion in that story. At the age of twenty-eight I would be cut from the Tennessee Titans on the account of an injury to my toe. Now, I know what you're thinking: *How is there going to be a lesson for my life out of a toe injury?* I get it, on the surface it might not seem like much. But underneath, the principles that are built around the experience can be applied to any physical injury.

To understand the purpose of what I am going to share with you, we must start at the beginning. My injury with the Titans— the turf toe that eventually got me cut from the team—didn't start in Tennessee. It didn't start back in Baltimore, either. That injury went all the way back to Ole Miss, to my first season with Ed Orgeron. We had just finished up a bad practice, and everyone was in the locker room, cooling off while we anticipated the next push from Coach O. Like clockwork, Coach came barreling in and told us to get back out there and do it all over again.

Of course, I didn't hesitate. I quickly laced up my cleats and ran back onto the field. I finished out the practice as hard as I could, just like Coach O asked. The problem was that our muscles had gotten cold. To go from sitting to a dead sprint is not wise from a muscular standpoint. But I wasn't going to have Coach think that I wouldn't do my best. My toe injury, the one that would take me out of Tennessee, started that day in Oxford, Mississippi. It wasn't that I actually hurt my toe. No, it was because I instilled in my mind the practice to push through, no matter the circumstance. I didn't take time to heal myself.

I'm sure every professional athlete has a similar tale. That's the strange power of sports at the highest level. The love and hate, the passion and frustration that push you to put the game before your body.

Even today, I'll look down at my biceps and notice the difference in my left and right arms. Because I never rehabbed it correctly after the tear, the scar serves as a reminder that I can push through the pain and still be able to perform. That, however, isn't always a good thing. Although being able to override the natural-born desire to quit is a hallmark of the greats, being able to know and respect your own limits is the key to setting yourself up for success.

When we are healthy, we feel invincible. We are more willing to push the boundaries, often overestimating our own strength. As soon as we are injured, reality sets in. The pain makes us clearly aware of the limitations of our body. Regret often follows.

Maintaining our strength for what is important is vital for achieving the goals we have set in life. No matter the physicality of the goal, no one will perform their best if their body isn't well. Something as small as a toe injury kept me from pursuing my goals with the Titans. As frustrating as that setback was at the time, it wouldn't even come close to touching the immensity of the struggle I would face when it came to my next injury.

I knew what was wrong when I hurt my toe. I knew what it needed—time to heal and rest. What would occur a few years later would be a completely different experience. I would face an injury that was almost invisible. One whose treatment wasn't as discernible.

· · ·

Mental injuries are like poisonous gas. They can't be seen. By the time you realize it's there, it's too late. Leaving it unchecked is dangerous, and for some it's deadly. It's a morbid analogy, but it's accurate.

When I was making my recovery in the NFL after being cut from the Titans, I was in a good spot mentally. I was in a routine. I was putting my head down and getting to work. My efforts were great. I had just come off a season ending in an appearance at the Super Bowl with the Carolina Panthers, when I would face one of my hardest walls yet.

The hit that caused my concussion would be a turning point in my life. I don't want to say that the whole event was unfortunate, because I am a believer that the value of life experiences is determined by what you make of them. What may seem bad at first can lead to something good if you let it. And something that is good in nature can lead to negative outcomes. All it takes is perspective and responsibility coupled with good character, and anyone can find a way to turn a bad situation good. This belief of mine would be tested to its limits in the experiences that followed that hit.

I shared with you the struggles that I had following the concussion. But what I would like to share now is the lesson I learned after having gone through that season of my life. I want to start a conversation around the topic of mental health. For too long it has been taboo to speak about it. That is something I have seen change in recent years, which is so important, especially given that maintaining one's mental health can be a matter of life or death.

When you think about it, the brain is the most powerful thing you've got. That is why you have to take care of it. You can rehab a muscle. You can set a bone. But the brain is intricate. Your mind is everything. We need to learn to be attentive and make choices that support its health.

To begin, we must acknowledge that the psychology of mental health is a tricky science. There is so much that we have only recently learned, and still much more that has yet to be discovered. One of the more recent revelations revolves around the effects poverty has on mental health. According to the CDC, people living below the poverty level are twice as likely to report serious psychological distress as those who live in conditions that are better by a factor of two. Put simply, those who lack the ability to care for themselves financially are also bound to experience mental health issues at an alarmingly higher rate. To me, that is the epitome of the saying "When it rains, it pours."

If you have your back against the wall, the odds that you are in a position or environment that is stress-inducing are even greater. That will put your mental health naturally at risk. So it's true when I say that our troubles often come to us in pairs. Very rarely are we afforded an opportunity or break in the storm to focus on our own health in a stable environment. Many of us have to face the realization that we need better care in our most desperate hours. That is why I say that the process of healing requires a helping hand. That is even more true when discussing issues surrounding mental health. This all begs the question we all so desperately have asked ourselves:

What am I supposed to do about it?

My answer is this: We need others to become better.

Counseling is an integral piece to healing. You need someone to talk to. Recently, I did an article with *People* magazine. I was quoted saying: "I bottled so much stuff up throughout my life. I carried that with me and I think it hurt me in the long run. That may be the only thing holding you back from being where you want to be—talking to somebody."

For me, that person was my best friend, Jamarca. He jokes that he is my lifeline—my phone-a-friend. Honestly, though, it's the truth. I have relied on him to be my sounding board so that I can verbalize my thoughts. It has helped me process so much, even helping me understand when I needed to address different treatment options for my mental health.

For the past few years, my battle for my mental health was very specific to me. It involved more than just an injury to the brain. It also forced me to face a lot from my childhood. That's why it was helpful to have someone to process all of that with. In particular it was helpful in discovering the right treatment options. At first, I didn't know enough about brain injury and chronic traumatic encephalopathy (CTE) to understand the dire nature of my situation, so I suited up the next week. There was no time to stop and see how I was truly feeling. When I finally realized there was a problem, I was put on a protocol to start my healing. By then it was too little, too late. The damage had already set in and escalated the process it would take to truly heal.

The point is, we all have different triggers and contributing factors, but when it comes to keeping our minds healthy, we've got to all land in the same place. Recognition of the problem, time and space to heal, and someone to talk to.

If you don't have a peer or a friend as selfless as Jamarca, that's okay. But don't let that stop you from finding somebody else to talk to, even if that means seeking out professional help. Today, more than ever, we have to find tools to help us cope. We have to take better care of each other. We have to ask the people we love the tough questions, like Jamarca did with me. If you have someone around you who's struggling, the words you say don't need to be profound. They just need to be earnest. A simple "Dude, are you okay?"

...

Needing help doesn't negate responsibility. At the end of the day your mental health becoming a priority is on you. Other people might not know what you are going through unless you say something.

When I finally did experience a season that required me to look inward and discuss my situation with someone I could trust, I struggled to come forward and speak up immediately. The mental conditioning of the game didn't encourage those kinds of behaviors. The pressures are enough for you as an athlete to build up your own walls and armor. At the pro level, you don't want to show any weakness. That is something that could invite ridicule in the locker room or, even worse, in the press.

As game day approached, the pressures of performing perfectly would begin to mount in the back of my head. When the time finally arrived to go out on that field, the thoughts would find their way front and center. Doubt, pressure, stress, anxiety: these were the normal emotions one would expect to experience with so much riding on one's shoulders. The expectations of an athlete at the professional level don't allow much room for grace. I knew that. That is why I would go silent on the eve of game day.

Before rushing out onto that field, I would revert inward. I kept my thoughts to myself. On the outside it might have looked like I was in the zone getting ready to leave it all out on the field. In truth I would be battling the flood of questions and doubts. It was my way of sucking it up and remaining strong.

The problem with that approach is that it doesn't leave room for grace. It doesn't leave room for you to be weak or admit when you need help. So when the time actually came for me to speak up and ask for help, I didn't know how to. I thought that was not acceptable as a professional athlete.

I do not believe I am the only professional athlete to have this experience. There have been countless others who have come forward in recent years to share their struggle and experience with the pressures of the game. That includes athletes from every sport. Whether they play on a field, court, track, green, or in a pool—whatever the space—the feeling was the same. *I can't let my opponent see any weakness.* Years of that kind of fortitude can wreck you. It taxes your mind. This kind of mental strain takes a toll. How each athlete has chosen to react to those mounting strains can vary. I've heard some of my favorite golfers—Tiger Woods and Bubba Watson—publicly speak about it. Terry Bradshaw, the former NFL quarterback turned TV announcer, has also talked about the substance abuse that stemmed from his depression. The list of athletes who have come forward on this issue is long and distinguished. From the stats, we know that at least 34 percent of elite athletes have struggled with this issue.

What does that tell you? If a professional athlete, who has trained their whole life building mental fortitude, can reach a breaking point, then so can you. Odds are, there are many people around you in the same exact boat. If you find yourself there alone, know that you have a choice. You can either run to vices that only delay addressing the problem while offering false and temporary relief, or you can choose to recognize the problem, admit you need help, and seek out someone you can trust to talk to about what those next steps should be.

It was when I did the latter that I began to see progress in my life. It was at that point that I started my journey to becoming a healthier me. Even though the conditions of my injury mean that I may never fully heal, I have put myself in a position where I can make the best decisions for myself and my family. When you bring yourself to a stabilized place, that is when you can survey the other walls facing you in life and address them accordingly.

. . .

Emotions are like the balance between the physical and the mental. They may not be tangible, but their presence can be felt and seen. After finding a lifestyle plan that has allowed me to prioritize my mental health, I was in a space that allowed me to address some of the other injuries I had received in my past. I'm not talking about a broken bone or a concussion. This time it involves the impact that behaviors and social systems can have on one's emotions.

Today's world looks wildly different from anything else we have ever encountered before. The emergence of social media has allowed many voices and opinions to be heard. While there is so much good that can come from that kind of a platform, the reality is, it can also be negative. More than the ability to give your opinion, the culture shift of today leads many to expect to hear your opinion on matters. That is doubly true if you are an athlete or celebrity. People think that if your job is being paid to entertain, then all forms of privacy should be denied. They expect to hear your opinion on current events and all matters of your life both personal and professional.

While I can agree that being paid to be in the spotlight requires some level of openness in a public forum, it is crucial to remember the natural boundaries that are necessary. These boundaries shouldn't just be options, they should be requirements for your own emotional health. What do I mean? I'm talking about limitations on what we share on social media. Let me explain how crucial this is by sharing how social boundaries helped me recover from my emotional injuries.

When I was facing the uphill battle of my exit from the NFL combined with the issue of my mental health, I was is in no state to help others. I had to put my health first and, in essence, that's exactly what I did. I pulled away from all my other unessential commitments to focus on getting better.

During that time, I made the tough decision to step away from social media. On top of the complexities of the brain, I was also forced to deal with many of the childhood traumas and the emotional scars they had left. Over the years, I felt the responsibility to be an example and guiding figure for others like me. Social media was the platform that allowed me to carry that torch beyond the NFL.

Thankfully, I didn't receive the backlash some other athletes did when choosing to be silent. Naomi Osaka would feel the full force of a world that expected her opinion when she refused to comment after the French Open in 2021. When that incident took place, I knew firsthand the potential reasons why Osaka did what she did. At the end of the day, we are human. It's only healthy to know when to set boundaries and step away.

As important as it may be to talk about your problems to someone you trust, it's just as important to not talk about them with everyone. Not everything needs to be public. By choosing to shrink the circle of people who I shared my personal life with to just Jamarca and my wife and kids, I gave myself the space to heal from my emotional wounds. I wasn't worried about the expectation of strangers. It was just me, my problems, and the people who loved me. It was exactly what I needed to get past the trauma that was resurfacing.

Once I came to a place where I felt I could stand on my own two feet, I began to slowly remove the boundaries set in place for my health. My reintroduction to social media was slow. I posted quotes and encouraging words from great writers, leaders, and thinkers, like Martin Luther King Jr. and Michael Jordan. It was my way of allowing others to speak the truths I wanted to say. It wasn't just my way of encouraging others again. It was also a way I could remind myself and give myself encouragement to continue forward in my healing process.

· · ·

The path forward reveals itself with healing. I think I am at a place where I can reenter the world I had to once step away from. I am ready to reengage from a position of strength. However, I still think this tool we all use today can be better. Many of us have hidden behind the veil to cast our opinions of criticism. I want to remind you that behind that phone, behind that app, and behind that profile are real people. People who can be hurt and who deal with anxiety just like every other human.

Before you post or comment, ask yourself, "Is what I say going to lead to something productive? Will the truth or my opinion lead to something that has positive or constructive change?"

If the answer is no, then I would challenge you to see the benefit of silence in that moment.

On the other hand, there is also a need for us to be more

comfortable having those uncomfortable conversations. Too many of us try to hide from the truth for fear of offense or discomfort. We may use the negative effects of "another person's truth" as a weapon to silence others, while we give ourselves free rein to hurl hate and criticism across the aisle to the other side. That is neither okay nor good. After all, no matter our beliefs, we are all human.

Look at Dr. Martin Luther King Jr., for example. He rose up and brought attention to an uncomfortable discussion regarding equality in our nation. Those discussions were so disruptive that they upended whole societies. However, even as hate was being volleyed at him, his approach and method of delivering that hard truth was done in love. It would be wise of us to follow his example in how we interact on social media. Let us speak truth in love when it possesses the potential to make this world a better place.

There may be times when you have to recognize that for your own health you need to set a boundary to step away from certain environments. It isn't a decision to remove yourself permanently from the world and other people. All it means is that you are giving yourself the space to heal and regain strength so that you may find yourself at a place where you can help others.

...

Of all the back-against-the-wall principles I want to share, this one is perhaps the most crucial: First, take care of your health. Everything else comes after.

If you are in a dark time right now, acknowledge what you are feeling. Seek help. Don't wait. Find that one person who truly listens to you. Ignoring the problem doesn't make it go away, and playing through the injury doesn't make you tough.

Once you do find those who are willing to walk with you on your journey to healing, take note of your surroundings. Know that it is to your benefit to set healthy boundaries during your season of healing, if it means that it gives you the space to recover. The last thing you need while trying to heal is input from the wrong influence. The idea is to protect yourself so you can regain the strength to face the other walls in your life with a clear mind.

In prioritizing your health, you will equip yourself with the best tools for overcoming other obstacles that lie before you—a strong mind and body.

15

#7: Your Answers Are in the Mirror

As I think about people trying to overcome the toughest odds—like the kids I hope to help at the Oher Foundation—I want to encourage them, but I also want to give them tools. I don't want to tell those kids things that will make them feel good in just the moment. I want my words to be useful over a lifetime.

One of these truths or principles I live by might be swimming against the tide, from a cultural standpoint. Nowadays we are quick to take pity, but slow to take responsibility. We make excuses, but even a good excuse is still an excuse.

Don't hear this as me lacking empathy. Life can be downright unfair. But what good will that do you if you are constantly dwelling on the bad hand you've been dealt?

There is *always* somebody who has it worse than you. You are living in a shed in Memphis? Well, some other guy is living under a bridge in Michigan—in December.

This is something I have talked about with foster kids. They, in particular, are deserving of some self-pity, but there comes a time when you have to put that down. It's not going to serve you. I'm not saying to ignore or lessen the pain you've experienced. As we talked about with mental health, you've got to cut yourself some slack. But at some point, you can't build anything worthwhile if you are unwilling to take some level of ownership. Even in an un-fair situation, you still have some responsibility. If you really think about that, it's empowering. It means there's something you can do for yourself. In back-against-the-wall situations, people often feel powerless.

If you have put in the effort and things still aren't going your way, you have to look yourself in the mirror and at least ask: *Am I the problem? Am I doing absolutely everything I can? Am I meeting help halfway?* This isn't like being in a sauna. There's no fog in front of that mirror. Your answers will be as plain as day.

The truth is, sometimes we don't want to know the answer. Because if we know, we have to do something about it. This hit me kind of hard during COVID. Part of my whole-body health will always involve maintaining a healthy weight. To put it bluntly, I care about my body. It's important to me to be in shape. Just like on the football field, I don't want to be average, I want to be phenomenal. From that first day at Granny White Park, I had worked hard and gotten down to a weight of 280 pounds. But then COVID hit, and as happens during a global pandemic, the excuses started slipping in. Masks and sheltering in place may be the prescribed cautionary actions against the virus, but they can also encourage you to stay in and neglect the routines that keep you active and healthy.

I had to practice what I preach. I looked in the mirror and got back on the train. I started at day one again.

This mindset has helped me countless times. Like when I got cut from the Titans. I had never been in a position where I did my best and couldn't perform to the level I expected. It was discouraging, but taking ownership removed the victim's mentality.

I looked myself in the mirror. Was it my fault? No, not necessarily. But it was still my responsibility. I did everything I could, but I could not get healthy. I couldn't get back to the caliber of play that was expected of me, so they had to make a business decision for the team.

The concept of taking ownership is one of the great things that sports in general can teach. At the end of the game, look up at the scoreboard and don't make excuses for what you see. Injury, weather conditions, the guy who was supposed to be blocking for you, even the ref—all of it fades away.

Take responsibility for the outcomes in your life.

This is something I want to put on the wall at my foundation. We've got to teach kids to stop making excuses and passing blame. We need to raise a generation who can be accountable. Look in the mirror. Respond to what you see.

...

The day that stranger came up to me in the park and asked to pray for me, I was at a low point. Physically, mentally, emotionally. I was under the greatest strain of my life, but what was most pressing on my mind at the moment was not the miles I had to go, but an incident that had happened a few weeks earlier.

Back then, it was hard to get me out of the house. The headaches and the light sensitivity, the disruptions to my sleep—all of those things had made me just want to stay in. I had yet to be medically released from the NFL, but all the signs were pointing to a very uncertain future for me.

Jamarca did his best to try to help me forget my current troubles and just lighten up. Laugh and have fun again. So one night in April 2017, we went out with a couple of guys to the comedy club.

The end result was something that still grieves me to this day. I had a run-in with an Uber driver that unfortunately got picked up by the media. The argument escalated into a scuffle, and suddenly there was a mug shot of me on BuzzFeed. Never in my life had I been somebody who hurts somebody weaker than me. Never in my life had I had trouble with authority, despite the fact that, when I was growing up, cops might have looked at me and assumed trouble.

So weeks later, when that stranger approached me at the park and asked who I was, I assumed he was going to comment on critical stories that had been written about me in the newspapers.

My response to the stranger—even though I had no idea what he wanted to talk about—was to be defensive. "Don't believe everything you read."

The reason for all that defensiveness: I was depressed. I'd been on the concussion protocol for months and months, and not only was I exhausted from being put on the shelf for an entire season, I was completely unsure of what was to come. I was still listening to the advice of my doctors and taking more medicines than I could count, and in light of that, I should not have had any alcohol, given my physical condition.

But what I didn't get to tell anyone was that the incident devastated me. Not only was I at the toughest point in my battle for my mind, I suddenly had to battle for my reputation. I wasn't sure I was up for it on top of everything I was already dealing with. I was lost, but more than that, I was angry.

I heard a good definition of anger during a sermon. The pastor was actually justifying it. He said, "It's okay to be angry. It's important to evaluate our anger. Anger is what we feel when something we love is threatened." I think his point was to show that anger can reveal the things that matter most to us. Depending on what you value, that can either be a righteous anger or a crippling one. What matters is how you choose to let the things you care about control your actions. Are they reactions or are they actions of passion and love that build up a better you or a better situation?

Many times, that anger is at the root of our anxiety and depression. The anger I felt that April was not just over the loss of everything, my entire life as I'd known it. When God made me, He gave me one thing that set me apart from everybody else: my mind. It was the only tool in my tool belt, but it was a powerful one. It got me out of tough situations. It was my rudder. Envisioning, doing the right thing, professing success—these were products of my mindset.

But the injury and the medications dulled that sensibility. They took my tool from me. For the first time in my life, I was in a hard spot and couldn't think my way out, and that left me angry.

That brain injury wasn't the first time when my anger stemmed from a threat. After the movie came out, the narrative downplayed some of the qualities that make me who I am. That I am self-taught. That I'm intuitive. That I work for things. The fictional story swept all of that away. It made it look like I was sitting there waiting for a handout. It cheapened those countless days of shaking off the cold and getting to class. The years of survival, resisting the streets, making the most of myself. For the sake of a better story, the movie suggested that some of the character traits that most define me are not true.

If anger is what you feel when something you love is threatened, then in both cases, my anger was warranted. So I felt it, but then I realized it was time to put it down. (By the way, that's Colin Powell's leadership principle number two.)

What you do in a moment of anger still has consequences. The charges might have been dropped, but the night of the Uber incident is something I have to take responsibility for, despite the circumstances that led to it. And Jamarca, as part of my true circle, realized that as well. He had to remind me of who I was. That very night, he called me out. "What's going on, Big Dawg? This isn't you. You never get mad like this."

A man takes ownership for his mistakes, and even in my haze, I knew that what Jamarca said was true. It wasn't me. It was my own first hard look in the mirror. I wasn't myself and I had to fix it.

Here's what I want you to take away: Whether you have made a mistake or things are just not going your way, you have to be willing to ask hard questions of yourself. You have to do a self-check first and see if you are your own problem.

When you've made a wrong turn, forgive yourself, but own up to it. Know that you are going to make mistakes. Some of them might even be big. The higher you are up the ladder, the harder it is to humble yourself, but it's never too late.

We can all look and find the fault of others in a situation. The truth is, the ones who can rise above a situation are the ones who can acknowledge their own hand in it. Their focus becomes bettering themselves and what they can control. I can acknowledge that sometimes you can face situations where you are not at fault. Many reading this book might have those experiences, whether it is being a victim of rape, abuse, or other violence. I don't mean to downplay the atrocities you experienced in those moments; this lesson might not fully apply for those experiences. My lesson is meant to be your way forward. It's a way to ensure that others don't get to lay a permanent hold on you. By taking responsibility for the things you can control, like your actions, reactions, thoughts, and character, and putting your focus on what you can do better there, you will find your way forward again.

Some of you might be saying, "What if I look in the mirror and I can't find the answers?"

Ask again. The answer will come in time. Before too long, you will begin to see the person you were meant to be. You take control of yourself and your life when you can humble yourself enough to see your faults, forgive them, and then change.

16

#8: Have Faith (A New Kind of Sunday)

I shared a story about Brodie Croyle when I started this book. Well, after he left the NFL, what he said to the press has stuck with me: "I'm about to go do something more important than just football."

The more time passes, the more I get what he was saying. I lived and breathed football because that's what it took to be great. But finally, I'm able to look up, I have some perspective. And there's no better representation of that than my Sundays.

It's crazy, but I think my body can still sense when it's Sunday. I wake up, and it takes me a minute. I go downstairs and pour myself a cup of coffee. I hear my wife and kids in the next room. I'm still kind of quiet on Sundays, but it's not in the way I used to be, with that tunnel vision I had to have to preserve my mindset before a game. Whether or not I'm sitting in a pew in church, I am intentionally quiet. I make space for family and downtime. I let Sundays be what they were designed to be—a day of rest. I still work out, but I deviate from the normal strenuous grind. I walk the track by my house. I climb the bleachers. I'm in my own head, reflecting on the week.

I think this might be my routine until I die. A quiet Sunday to make up for all the years of intense ones. I get that's not very exciting, and I'm fine owning that.

My own faith has had an interesting course. Even when I was on the streets, I recognized that I could not control everything. As a kid, I wouldn't have an opportunity to attend church on a regular basis like many within my community, but my relationship with God was present nonetheless. My faith was more than just a building or a way you're supposed to act. I believed in something—a higher power—even before I had a name for it. Even if I wasn't sure it worked, I prayed.

Today, if I call you family or a friend, I pray for you. I am loyal that way. Pastor Dale, after we had been friends for a while, noticed this about me. We were sitting in his office one day, dreaming, discussing what would become the Oher Foundation, when he said, "Michael, this might sound weird to you, but I feel like I found a verse that is the theme of your life."

"What's that?" I asked. "And if you say something about Goliath, I'm going to come at your head."

"No." He laughed. "There was a verse I was reading in the New Testament the other day. It says, 'I'm the Good Shepherd. The Good Shepherd sacrifices his life for his sheep.'"

"Okay . . ." I raised my eyebrows.

"Well, we know that passage is talking about Jesus. And at face value, we know it has nothing to do with you and everything to do with God. But part of our maturity as Christians is to become more like Christ. And, Mike, this is the way you are like him. You are a protector. You are a shepherd. You gravitate to the weak."

Pastor Dale went on to read the rest of the passage. "'A hired hand will run away when he sees the wolf coming. He will abandon the sheep because they don't belong to him.'"

This hit me pretty hard. When it came down to the foundation and the kids, Dale was right—I wasn't a hired hand. If needed, I would lay down my life for these kids I was trying to help.

If I go back to my anger test and ask myself what was threatened, the answer again comes down to my intellect. My loyalist tendencies were used in making me look simple.

But that verse in John brought me back again. To the real me. To the protector I felt like God had always meant for me to be.

. . .

Sunday used to be a day to go to war. Today, regardless of whether I make it to church or not, it is a day of intentional rest.

As I said in the opening, we are at a unique time in history. We are looking for hope. According to Pew Research, prayers doubled in the past year alone. Whatever you believe, it is a scientific fact that prayer calms the nervous system, shuts down fight or flight, and increases pain tolerance and immunity. Point being, there is value in prayer beyond what you might think.

Those facts are all well and good. Maybe hearing some of them will convince even the most reluctant to try out releasing control. Honestly, that is part of what faith has meant for me. My entire life, everything has been on my shoulders. There is so much pressure everywhere you turn, and that pressure can break you.

But if we take a step back, we'll recognize that some things are beyond our control and even our understanding.

There are miracles out there, and they vary in size. But you won't see them unless you *want* to see them. I'll leave you with one of mine.

. . .

MJ started playing T-ball last year. Of all the milestones I've waited for as a father, getting to spend time with my son and coach him in sports was top on the list. Since he was already six years old, I knew we were getting started a little late. I try to model my relationship with my son the same way I wished it had been for me if I'd had a father who could have been present. I expect and push for greatness, but I also leave room for reassuring love. That is how I approach my time with MJ in sports as well.

Before the season actually started, we had a Zoom call with the team, and we got to meet my son's first coach, a scraggly-haired guy named Judd Granzow.

Immediately, I liked Judd's vibe. He was soft-spoken but also kind of intense. He wore a hoodie and a small earring, making him less clean-cut than the other types in our current Crieve Hall neighborhood of Nashville. I could dig that.

A few weeks later, we had an in-person barbecue for the team, and Coach Judd walked over and said hello to me.

"What's up, Michael?" We'd only seen each other online, but he acted like an old friend.

I shook his hand.

"How are things going, man?" Coach Judd had this weird kind of smile about him. He looked me in the eye like he was genuinely interested. There was something familiar about his eyes. They were so blue and intense. For a second, I started to panic like I sometimes do. *Oh Lord, here we go again. This guy is too nice. He's probably wanting me to invest in some business venture.*

I hate that that's my reaction, but when you are constantly being hit up when you're just trying to do something normal (like watch your son's T-ball game), you can't help it.

But I was way wrong. Come to find out, Coach Judd was in ministry. He worked as an assistant pastor at a local church. Judd himself had some serious athletic pedigree. He was drafted by the Dodgers in the 1990s and played two seasons of Minor League Baseball before he switched over to football and won a national championship as a linebacker for Tennessee. After his own career was over, he started to train athletes. He helped launch a couple of private training facilities in Nashville, one of them preparing guys for the NFL Combine.

"We hit it out of the park with this guy," I told Tiffany later on. "I don't know how we got a guy of this caliber. Like having Jerry Rice coach your Little League."

The answer, as I'd come to find out, was that Judd was as selfless as he was gifted. His son had finished up high school sports, and since no one was willing to step up and coach a seven-year-olds' traveling team, he raised his hand, even though he didn't have a kid in the league.

I finished up my barbecue and thanked Coach Judd for his efforts and told him we'd see him on the diamond.

. . .

Roll ahead a few months and I was invited by a friend at the gym to speak to Brentwood High School's football team. They had made it far—all the way to the state championship—and the speaker they'd booked had canceled at the last minute.

"Nothing like being second-string," I joked with my friend.

But I was honestly happy to do it. Especially when I learned Coach Judd was also chaplain of the Brentwood football team. My son had been having an amazing season. His game and even his attitude had changed with Coach Judd's influence, so I figured it was the least I could do after what he'd done for us.

At that point, I hadn't really done a lot of public speaking. Definitely not since my "comeback."

It was strange to think about myself as someone who could inspire others. Back in the NFL, one of the greatest moments for me was hearing those pep-up speeches before the game, and now I was getting to be on the other side of that.

I looked down at those faces gathered in the locker room. I was a little surprised by the attention they gave me. They were quiet and listening. At that time, I didn't know a lot of high school boys, and I thought most of them were punks. This actually wasn't the first time I'd seen the team. In fact, I'd seen them hundreds of times. Brentwood High School is connected to Granny White Park. I'd watched those guys during my own workouts. Strange as it sounds, I had a connection with them. They reminded me of myself back at Briarcrest, and because of that, they were part of my motivation to get back to health.

"Every play is important," I told them. "Every rep counts. You know, I used to walk that park right over there. I was trying to get back in shape. I would climb the bleachers, and when I took a break, I would see you guys practice, putting in the work, and now look at you, at the championship. That time you put in is paying dividends."

I paced around like I was Denzel in *Remember the Titans*. "I saw you after practice, too. All you guys burning out of the parking lot in your trucks."

The kids all laughed at that.

"My point is—people are always watching you. What you are made of is the sum of these decisions. I've got a lot of respect for you guys and your program. People are cheering you on, so go out there and give it your all today."

• • •

After the game, it was raining when Judd walked with me across the Brentwood High School parking lot to my truck.

"Thanks again for speaking, dude," he said.

"Man, it was fun," I said. "But too bad we didn't win. If I'm going to be a pregame motivator, I'm going to need the outcome of my speeches to be more wins than losses."

"We'll work on those stats." Judd laughed.

We were both standing there getting wet, so I was about to climb in my truck when Judd said, "Michael, I gotta ask. Do you remember when we first met?"

"Uhh . . ." I thought for a second. I had no idea. And also, it was a strange question. "I guess at the field . . . or maybe the team barbecue?"

He shook his head. "No, it was right over there." He pointed to the parking lot by the slope in the walking path. "I prayed for you one day when you were at the park."

"Oh my gosh." I paused. "That's why you are familiar to me. *You're* the guy. The stranger who prayed for me. I remember now," I said.

Judd smiled, seeing the memory kind of wash over me.

Now that I know Judd, I know this is how the man operates. It's like he has a radar for people who are hurting, who need encouragement. We go to the mall, and we might walk by a hundred people, and he seems to sense out the ones who need to be spoken to that day. That hot day in July 2017, that person was me.

"It's funny because I *really* didn't want to pray for you." Judd laughed again.

He went on to explain how it happened. "After I saw you, I felt led to do something, but I didn't want to bother you. I know how you guys are. You've been in the NFL; you just don't want to be bothered."

"You're right. I was working out alone for a reason," I said, laughing.

So he didn't. He told God sorry, finished up the team workout, got in his car, and left.

"But this is the craziest part of the story," Judd said. "For ten years, every time I left Brentwood, I took a left to go home. Without fail. But that day, for whatever reason, I took a right."

Of course, that made Judd annoyed with himself. It had been a long day. It was hot. It was time to go home and check on his wife and kids, but again, he felt a tug on his heart: *You need to go pray for that guy.*

So Judd, being the good Christian that he is, cut a deal with the Lord. "Fine, I will drive back to the park. If he is there, I'll stop and pray for him."

More than an hour had passed since he'd seen me, so he felt like it might be a safe bet. "I'm sure he's gone," Judd said to himself.

But there I was, on my last lap, covered in sweat.

"So why did you do it?" I asked him. "What made you so certain I needed help?"

"I couldn't ignore the compassion Jesus gave me," he said. "I felt God pulling me to you. It was as if He was telling me to show you the same compassion He had given me."

Remember what I said about my circle never changing? Well, when you meet people like Judd, you make an exception.

•••

I don't pretend to have a lot of spiritual knowledge, but I think the Lord loves a good coincidence.

Turns out, Judd was involved in bringing parts of my life together in another way.

Judd was the man in the staff meeting when Pastor Dale said he wanted to start a school. Judd had overheard me talk about my passion for educating underprivileged kids, so he was the one who set up that meeting with me and Pastor Dale. All the ways our lives intersected, I'd have to agree with Dale on this one: "It's a God thing."

Our friendship grew. What I appreciated about Judd is that he had the kind of depth and understanding of what it took to make great athletes, but for him, all of those outside skills were a distant second to what he really wanted to build: the hearts of men.

Judd invited me to a men's Bible study on Friday mornings. That was not something I'd been a part of since Briarcrest, but as I was just coming out of a long season of struggling alone, the connection to the group seemed like a good thing.

Fast-forward several months and Judd offered to let me lead one of the Friday studies. He didn't just offer. He gave me a big nudge. The kind of nudge that just makes you go ahead and do it, even if you're not sure what you're doing. Even if you're not sure you want to.

At the time, we'd been following along in the New Testament and we were in the book of Mark. It just so happened that the story I was supposed to lead was Jesus healing the leper. We were moving chronologically, so it wasn't like Judd had handpicked that story for me because he knew my background. I thought it was interesting that of all the stories in the Bible, the one that fell on me had to do with a dramatic—miraculous—healing.

I'm not a preacher, so basically I just shared what I could see. Leprosy, as most people might know, is a pretty awful disease. It was one that was not taken lightly. A leprous person was a lonely person. Outside of the colony, there was no connection. Their pain, in general, was understood by themselves alone.

In the story, when he saw the leprous man, it says Jesus was "moved with compassion." When I did a little research, I found that the use of the word *compassion* in the Greek language is not just plain old sympathy. It is deep anguish; it's a word that is associated with the guts of a person. Jesus didn't just feel bad for the guy, he was broken for him.

In my study, I also learned a few things about lepers. For one, they were so shut out and so unwelcome, they would have to announce themselves before they approached a crowd.

"Unclean!" they'd have to yell. "Away from me!"

Knowing all that liability, Jesus could have simply used his words to heal the guy. He would have sent in the check and kept his distance. But instead, he "came near" to someone who was suffering. He actually touched him. Even though that closeness could have meant danger for himself, at worst. Discomfort at best. "I am willing," he said. "Be clean." By Jewish law, just in doing this, Jesus himself would have been "unclean."

I think I'd heard that story before, but I'd thought about it in a kid sort of way. Lepers wrapped up like mummies and all that. But as an adult, it was pretty powerful to me. It's funny how once you have experienced desperation for yourself, you see the pain of others with new eyes.

That nearness was what I wanted in my legacy. It was what was missing in my own childhood—*He came near.*

Nearness was my calling at the Oher Foundation. Putting myself in someone's bad situation so that I could make a difference. Seeing a kid who might otherwise go unseen. I could sit in my house and write checks to worthy organizations all day long— and there's a place for that—but God moved in my heart and brought me to a place of compassion. He called me to be the shepherd who stayed when the hired hands ran away.

So I guess you could say that these days I am a person of faith. You can't have the life that I've had—the triumphs and the pains—and not see the invisible hand of a power much greater than mortal man. That power sustained me as a kid before I had any support.

It healed my mind as a grown man.

It humbles and guides me even today.

Recently someone reminded me of an old saying: *There are no atheists in the trenches.* I know that was true in my life. When things are going well, we feel like we don't need anything. We are in control, in the driver's seat. But weakness makes us stop and look up.

In your brokenness—in your back-against-the-wall moments—you have an opportunity to try out faith. The God I've come to know doesn't scoff at the weak. He will be near when everyone else sends you away.

When you have tried everything else and nothing is working, try praying.

I would bet my Super Bowl ring that He'll meet you halfway.

17

#9: I Shouldn't Be a Miracle
(Have a Mission)

The last principle I want to share is simple: *Have a mission.* One of the best ways out of hard times is to serve something greater than yourself. I'm not reinventing the wheel here, but if the play leads to a touchdown, you run it. Again, and again.

I started out this book talking about legacy and how I feel privileged that I have the time to think about that while I'm still young. Believe me, I understand what it's like to be caught in the grind each day, just trying to put food on the table and get by, but I want to suggest that if you are reading this, there is someone out there who needs help. Your help.

In my previous book, I talked about my hopes for my football career, and believe me, those goals I achieved and victories I won felt good. But ultimately, I've come to realize that the deepest satisfaction and purpose comes alive when you find a mission that is bigger than yourself. This principle is embodied in a singular vision that has only just recently become a reality. I want to share the story about how I was able to bring my vision to life in my renewed mission in education.

...

For almost half my life now I've heard these words: "Man, it's a miracle you made it out of the hood."

And always, I've nodded my head earnestly. "I know—thank God!" I've told them—and I've meant it.

As I said in my previous book, the odds were against me, no doubt. The odds are still against kids stuck in their own "Hurt Villages" across America.

Call it providence. Call it luck. A little of both. But I broke the cycle. It's been a couple of decades since I've spent a night in the projects, but I haven't forgotten what it was like. That nagging hollow feeling in your stomach when you're truly hungry. It is all-consuming. You can think about nothing else. And that kind of panic when you start to see the sun getting lower in the sky and it's cold out, and you don't know where you're going to sleep that night. When the morning finally found me curled up somewhere—in a shed, on a porch, in a car—I didn't know what the day was going to bring, but I knew one thing was a guarantee: struggle. Struggle to find something to eat. Struggle to find a ride. Struggle to find a place to stay. Literally nothing was easy. It was the mental equivalent of treading water. My mind had to be constantly pushing against the obstacles or I would just sink. But what got me through those hard times was dreaming of the day when I could stop treading and just rest. Just for one day.

I was at my house not too long ago when I heard some water dripping from the kitchen. It was just the dishwasher leaking, but it caused sort of a flashback. Incidents from my past never stay buried. They're always coming back to me, sometimes when I least expect them. Looking at the puddle on the hardwood kitchen floor, I remembered a night from my childhood that I hadn't thought about in a long time. Our apartment had flooded. Of course it was just us kids at home, so there was nothing we could do about it. I had a bed at the time, but it was just a mattress on the floor, so it got soaked. That night I went to sleep staring at the water, hoping it wouldn't reach the edge. Kind of traumatic for a six-year-old.

When I look at where I am today in light of that moment, I have to admit, yes, it is a miracle that I broke the cycle. That my son, by the grace of God, won't ever have to experience a night like my worst nights on the streets.

But here's the news flash: It shouldn't be that way.

Now that I'm older, every time I hear those words I want to say, *I shouldn't be a miracle!*

It's time to stop thinking of it in that context. Let's not have the mindset that getting out of the hood (or whatever you want to call it) is doing the impossible. A miracle is falling off a boat in the middle of the ocean and getting found five days later. Not a kid from the inner city getting an education, a decent job, and a home outside of the projects.

There are a lot of statistics that support the "I'm a miracle" argument. I grew up in North Memphis, and at one time it was the poorest zip code in the country. Things looked bleak for kids in our neighborhood. We were told that we only had a 47 percent chance of graduating high school. And college? There was only a 5 percent chance of that, even if you were working hard and doing all the right things.

I read a national statistic that said by the end of primary school, a student who received free meals is estimated to be three terms behind their peers. By age fourteen, that average jumps up to five terms behind. The reason why? Hunger is a huge distraction! How can you learn when you are too hungry to even think? It is impossible to focus on the future when you're just trying to get from one day to the next.

So while the current data might suggest a miracle, I am making it my mission to do what is in my power to change that. Success stories for urban kids simply should not be a miracle.

Not being a miracle also means that sports are not your ticket out. For the Oher Foundation, we also wanted to get another thing straight. The opportunities we provide wouldn't be just for athletes. In considering enrollment for kids in what we are calling the Opportunity Program, we knew we wanted to look inside, not out. At hearts. To find the boys and girls who wanted the opportunity. It would be our way of putting first things first. Like the passage Pastor Dale is always quoting: "Seek first *His* kingdom and *His* righteousness *and then* all these things will be added to you."

But with underprivileged kids, people often get it backward. They say they want to help urban youth, but it's not really until they see athletic potential that anyone will pour into them. I knew that I wanted the Oher Foundation to be the opposite of that. I wanted the kids we found to know that they are here because those around them believe in them simply because of the witness of their character in action and not because of their stats on a field.

In a lot of ways, the kids we reach our hands out to won't be so different than the little Michael Oher who was looking for his one big opportunity. At the heart of my success was the determination and will that I instilled in my mind from day one. It didn't matter how much talent I had athletically. If I hadn't made the choice to be someone with good, dependable character who was willing to work my way through school with academics being a priority, I wouldn't be where I am today. I want to find those kids who are making the right choices and who have the attitude to become great, but are simply lacking the resources and support to make a difference. Instead of professional athletes, I hope to reach into the heart of inner cities everywhere and pull out the leaders, lawyers, doctors, and engineers of tomorrow.

....

When I set out to do something, it is almost more fun if that thing is considered impossible.

The dream of the Oher Foundation fits into that category. The first time I met with the governor's office, I was told these words: "Mr. Oher, I'm not saying it can't happen, but with a project this size, involving so many different facets and organizations, rules and legislation, you're looking at about thirty meetings before you can even get started—minimum."

And my response was simple. "Well, let's consider this one of thirty."

The room laughed, but I was serious. I thought back to football practices in the summer in Mississippi, when my body was pouring sweat and my legs hurt so badly that I could barely stand up.

"I can go to meetings," I told the governor's team. "It's not like someone's hitting me."

The Oher Foundation is just now getting started. It took a couple of years to get it planned out and going, but I can say with confidence that we are now at a spot where we can actually engage with kids and make a difference. But just because we are now operating inside our first school doesn't mean the hard part is over. I'm still talking to folks and taking meetings. Showing up, shaking hands. Meeting kids like Kinnedy. Keeping good working relationships with the people who've joined us along the way. In all honesty, as long as there is funding, I won't stop thinking of ways we can reach and impact more kids' lives for the positive through education.

At first my vision was just an idea, but then other people started getting involved. Judd, Pastor Dale, Highland Park Church, the Sparks Foundation, and even Vanderbilt University had a part to play. Before I knew it, I was in the living rooms of some of the heaviest hitters in the Nashville financial community and they're telling me they want to help. That's what happens when you surround yourself with like-minded dreamers. They go with you and help you grow your vision.

It all started with a simple goal: *How can I help the next Michael Oher? How can I make sure that one kid has a better path?*

With the Oher Foundation, I'm using all these principles I've shared with you. It's a massive undertaking, and it's a mission with a never-ending goal. As long as there are kids who need help, I will be there to provide the opportunity. I'm seeing this through. I'm not sure how far I can take it. Maybe it's just Nashville, or maybe I can take it across every city in America. Either way, this mission is going to be my legacy. It will be more defining (and hopefully more lasting) than any Oscar-winning movie or any win on the football field—even a Super Bowl. Like the old song says: "If I can help somebody as I travel along the way, my journey will not be in vain."

This is a new season in my life. I understand how quickly time goes, so I have set my missions out in front of me. Now that I've faced my walls, one of them is speaking again. I am going and seeing folks across the country, sharing with them these lessons. I've learned and humbly listened to their stories afterward. The invitations come from all over. They are as diverse as the fan mail I still get in my Facebook message box. I'm invited into every circle, from business executives to homeschool moms. Sports programs and churches. There is even discussion of an Ole Miss commencement speech.

Who would have thought, ten years ago in Baltimore—when I was praying that nobody would ask me any questions about my past—that one day I would climb a stage in front of strangers for an impromptu Q&A?

Recently I got to do something pretty special—visit my old

friend Coach Freeze at Liberty University in Lynchburg, Virginia. I spoke to the Boys and Girls Club there, sharing some of the principles I've shared with you in this book.

After the speech I went to dinner with Coach Freeze and his wife, Mrs. Jill. It was so good to be with people who know me. To laugh and reminisce about old times. But I have to say, it was emotional, too. Looking across the dinner table at me, Mrs. Freeze kept tearing up, thinking about how far I'd come from those first days at Briarcrest. It was hard for her to believe that I was that same kid who sat at her dining room table eating shrimp alfredo.

Leonardo DiCaprio said something I think is very true: "Every next level of your life will demand another you."

The guarded kid who felt most comfortable in the periphery is taking center stage, because that's what my calling is at the moment. It's still me, it's just the next-level me.

What about you?

What is the next-level "you" going to look like?

I want to tell you what I told those kids back at Big Oak Ranch.

There is power in your mind. More power than you can possibly dream at this point. So, whatever you want your future to be, you've got to change your thoughts right now.

...

What does that next step look like for you? After every storm there is a new day. The sun will eventually shine on your horizon. It is the reward you get for standing up to face your troubles head-on.

As you take those steps forward, you will begin to feel the distance you put between yourself and the walls you had once found your back against. As the obstacles begin to clear, you will have open reign over the direction you take your life. Even if you might not have the opportunities of an ex–NFL player, you will have the opportunity of choice. What does that mean? That means that beyond your walls is the power and opportunity for you to choose the life you want to live and the legacy you will choose to leave behind.

Begin to ask yourself this question: *What do I want my mission to be beyond the walls?*

There is no one reading this book who doesn't possess the power or ability to shape the character of their own mind and heart. Everyone has the ability to make a difference for the better.

My choice was made to help those like me through the tool of education. Maybe your mission is to simply be a better father, husband, mother, or wife. Or maybe your mission is as bold as feeding the hungry. Whatever it may be, if the heart of your action is good and you instill in yourself the character to persevere, you have the ability to make positive change in this world.

Just imagine if everyone chose to live like this after facing their own walls in life. Many of the kids coming up in today's world might not have to face some of the walls we had to. That's what this book is for. It's a guiding light in how to approach and move beyond the walls of hardship we often create for ourselves and others.

My hope is that this book has been of some benefit to you, if at the very least it has encouraged you to take that first step in finding your path forward again.

Maybe I will find you on the other side of your walls, ready to make a change for good in this world alongside me.

Epilogue

I started this book talking about encouragement, and that is where I want to end. That is why I would like to use the space on these last couple pages to discuss with you the basis of what we are doing at the Oher Foundation to help fill the gaps for kids in education.

OHER FOUNDATION

Our Mission

The Oher Foundation seeks to elevate socioeconomically disadvantaged youth by providing them with opportunities to escape the cycle of poverty and hopelessness through higher education, mentorship, and healthy living.

Today, the Oher Foundation is partnering with schools and organizations in the Nashville, Tennessee, area, bringing opportunities in education to the kids who need it most. By working with people within the foster system, we are able to identify kids who show the potential to excel academically. For many, success in the classroom is only limited by the lack of support a student might have outside the classroom. We seek to fill those gaps of support in a program we have devised and call the Opportunity Program.

For the students hungry for success, the Opportunity Program provides more than just a scholarship to a school able to meet their learning needs. We believe in the commitment that others made in my life, and we seek to mimic their commitment to the students we help. On top of scholarships, we also provide long-term life mentors, enrichment opportunities, emotional and mental support, as well as all the necessary resources to become academically successful. This includes items like clothing, food, transportation, and program fees like learning assessment testing.

To learn more about the efforts we are making to ensure that my story isn't just a miracle but a reality for others just like me, visit www.oherfoundation.org.

Those who feel inspired to support our cause and change a life may donate online at www.oherfoundation.org to support a student.

Acknowledgments

It is such a gift that the team that helped share the story of *I Beat the Odds* a decade ago came back together to create an update to that story. And this book is better because the team expanded!

Some of those who helped with both making my story happen and then helping to share it include: Robert and Tracy Sparks, who supported me from Briarcrest to the launching of the Oher Foundation; Tony Henderson, who took me in and made my ability to receive a great education possible; Coach John Harrington from Briarcrest, who put me on the track to pursue a career in football and standing as a strong example of what a man should be; Brodie Croyle, who lived his life in a way that served as the inspiration for me to find my purpose in helping kids like me.

A special shout-out is also due to Quintero, Anthony, and Dell Borrow. It was in my junior year of high school with you all when I really started to excel in athletics. I was able to become the player I was, because of you all opening your home where you fed and clothed me—that really started the trajectory moving in the right direction! Because of it, I would become an all-American football player and started to learn the true meaning of family.

I also owe so much of this story to teammates and leaders from my NFL experiences with the Baltimore Ravens, Tennessee Titans, and Carolina Panthers. I specifically want to mention Matt Birk, a wise mentor who encouraged the best of me and led by example for me to become a selfless leader both on and off the field; Coach John Matsko, another mentor who taught me so much, not just for the game but for lessons in life; and Dave Gettleman, who allowed me to extend my career in the NFL and play for the Panthers when so many had given up on me.

But no teammate has helped me grow like Jamarca Sanford, a genuine friend who stood by me no matter what my status was or where I was in life. He has always been someone I can share the ups and downs with and count on.

When it came to crafting this story, getting it all down accurately and truthfully, I want to thank my writer and friend Don Yaeger. We did this ten years ago and stayed together as friends, which allowed this book to happen. And this entire project got even better when Walker Petty, who also helps me with the Oher Foundation, threw himself into it. Our agent Ian Kleinert also was a great teammate.

The publishing team at Penguin Random House, led by Megan Newman, Lindsay Gordon, and Hannah Steigmeyer, took what we wrote and made it so much better. Again, they believed in me ten years ago and believed in this book, too. It is hard to find real loyalty in this world, but they define it!

Last—but *absolutely* not least—this book doesn't happen without my amazing family. It all starts with my wife, Tiffany, a strong supportive partner in life who has pushed me to be a better man. I am so thankful for the family and life we have built together. Then Kobi and Kierstin, bringing you in as my own taught me patience and helped me grow into the man I respect today. With you I have grown so much. And the two greatest gifts in my life, MJ and Naivi. My greatest accomplish-ment in life has been bringing you into this world and raising you in a way that was not possible for me. I want to give you the life I wish I had growing up. Your existence brings so much love and purpose into my life.